UNFORGETTABLE DEVILS

GAMES & MOMENTS FROM THE PRESS BOX, ICE & FRONT OFFICE

MATTHEW BLITTNER

ISBN: 978-0-578-56963-5
ISBN-13: 978-0-578-56963-5

DEDICATION

In this world, it's not enough to merely believe in yourself. Rather, you need others to believe in you as well.

To that end, this book would not have been completed without the support of my family and friends.

Specifically, I'd like to dedicate this book to my parents -- Mandi and Seth -- and sister Tara for their constant support even during the toughest times. And to my friends -- Arianna Rappy, Stef Hicks, Leanna Gryak, Maggie Wince, Walt Bonné, Daniel Greene, Jared Fertig, Jason Russo, Peter Koutros and Robert DeVita -- who were always there for me when I needed them and I thank them for that.

CONTENTS

INTRODUCTION

It's never easy to enter a new market. And it's even harder when that market is already saturated with competitors.

But that is the harsh reality the New Jersey Devils faced when they uprooted themselves from Colorado (at that time they were known as the Rockies) and touched down in New Jersey as the newly christened Devils.

While the Garden State was devoid of a National Hockey League team, it was in close proximity to New York, which housed two NHL franchises -- the New York Islanders and the New York Rangers, who also happened to be an Original Six team.

So, what chance at success did the Devils have? Especially when one considers that this wasn't their first move, as the franchise was originally born the Kansas City Scouts before making its way to Colorado.

However, they did have one thing going for themselves and that was an owner who desperately wanted his team to be taken seriously in its' new home.

Dr. John McMullen decided to focus solely on the New Jersey market and to ignore New York, something his NFL counterparts with the Jets and Giants refused to do.

But it proved to be a stroke of genius as the Garden State fans embraced having a team all to their own.

Unfortunately, the first several years were lean ones. The team wasn't competitive and there were only sporadic glimpses of greatness.

However, that soon changed, for the Devils made a mad dash to the playoffs during the 1987-88 season. A late season surge had them positioned to make the playoffs for the first time in franchise history. But it wouldn't be easy.

They needed EVERY. LAST. POINT. to qualify for Lord Stanley's grueling tournament. And thanks to some overtime heroics from John "Mac" MacLean, they secured that coveted spot.

The playoffs weren't easy and nobody expected the Devils to go all the way, but they did treat their fans to a number of memorable moments -- including the mysterious "Yellow Sunday" incident.

(Did Head Coach Jim Schoenfeld really tell Referee Don Koharski to eat another donut? And did he push him or did Koharski just trip?)

From there, the Devils spent the next few seasons building themselves up as a Stanley Cup contender. And by the time the 1993-94 season was underway it seemed they FINALLY had what it would take to hoist the storied Stanley Cup.

However, one team stood in their way -- the New York Rangers.

The Devils finished the regular season with an eye-popping 106 points! But the Rangers outdid them with 112, a number that was inflated by the Blueshirts' 6-0 mark against New Jersey in the regular season.

These two teams were on a collision course to meet in the post-season and when they began the Eastern Conference Final -- each just four wins away from playing for the Stanley Cup -- New Jersey felt it had what it would take to topple the Rangers.

And that feeling was further intensified when the Devils took a 3-2 series lead and headed into Game 6 at the Meadowlands with a chance to close out the series and their cross-river rivals.

The Devils even took a 2-0 lead in the first period, leading New Jersey defenseman, Ken Daneyko to later say that he remembered the Rangers looked like they were done.

And while a magical night ensued, it wasn't the Devils who benefitted, as Blueshirts' captain, Mark Messier delivered on his "Guarantee" with a third period natural hat-trick (part of a four point night) to force Game 7. And when New York put away New Jersey in double-overtime, the Devils' dreams had officially been dashed.

But New Jersey's Devils didn't let that loss deter them. Nor did they let the NHL's lockout ruin their resolve. Rather, the Garden Staters again qualified for the playoffs in the 1994-95 season. And this time, they weren't going to fall short against anyone!

The team marched to the Stanley Cup Final, where it faced the powerhouse Red Wings (another Original Six franchise).

And nobody gave them a snowball's chance in hell to knockoff Detroit. In fact, one hockey pundit boldly declared that the Red Wings would beat New Jersey in three straight and that the Devils would forfeit Game 4.

But perhaps it was the Red Wings who should have forfeited Game 4, as they lost the first three games of the series and generally looked like the lesser team.

There was just no stopping this Devils' train.

New Jersey controlled the play in Game 4 (just as it had throughout the series) and by the time the last few seconds drained off the clock at the end of the third period -- and the clock read 0.00 -- the Devils were finally Stanley Cup Champions.

Meanwhile, two years later, the Devils had another memorable playoff moment. And it was authored by goalie, Martin Brodeur, who scored a goal during their 1997-playoff series against Montreal.

Yes you read that right. A goalie scored a goal in the PLAYOFFS!

Of course, over the next several years the Devils were a constant presence among the league's elite, they even captured two more Cup trophies in 2000 and 2003.

But eventually even the greatest dynasties fall. Luckily for the Devils, their fall was slow and steady, rather than abrupt.

From 2004-2019 New Jersey won a grand total of zero Cups, but it wasn't for lack of trying.

And along the way, they fashioned some absolutely unforgettable moments, including Brodeur's march towards history.

For many years hockey analysts had predicted that Brodeur would eventually break Patrick Roy's hallowed record of 551 career wins. And when the 2008-09 season began, Marty was within striking distance.

It was no longer a question of IF he would break Roy's record, but WHEN?

And it was all the sweeter for Brodeur, who grew up a huge Montreal Canadiens fan and idolized Patrick Roy.

As the season wore on, Brodeur continued his steady pace and shortly after the calendar flipped to 2009, he was finally on the doorstep of history.

He needed JUST. ONE. WIN to tie the record -- two to break it. And what better way for him to make history than to face off against his idol's former team and his boyhood team -- with Roy and his family in attendance to boot!! And in their own house no less?!

But as they say, records are meant to be broken and on a cold winter night in Montreal, Brodeur equaled Roy with a 3-1 victory.

The Devils were jubilant for sure, but there was still work to be done. Brodeur may have tied Roy, but he still needed one more win to call the record his own. And there was a problem.

It was St. Patrick's Day in the States and the Blackhawks were coming to New Jersey for a game, a potentially record-breaking one. But if Brodeur failed to get the win against Chicago he likely wouldn't get another chance to set the record at home, for after the game, the Devils were leaving for a multi-city road trip, which meant, if he didn't get win No. 552 at home, he was going to get it on the road, where he would be subjected to hostile crowds.

And it was very important to Brodeur and his teammates that he get the win at home.

From the moment Brodeur took the ice in Newark he was serenaded with chants of, "Mart-tee, Mart-tee, Mart-tee." And when he made a beautiful, game-saving pad save on a last second shot from Troy Brouwer, the record was finally his, thus setting off a raucous celebration.

Meanwhile, as Brodeur continued to pile up the accolades there was one thing he seemingly couldn't attain -- a fourth Stanley Cup championship.

As the new decade began, Brodeur's legendary teammates moved on, some to other teams and most to retirement. So, if Marty and Co. were to once again taste the sweet nectar of champagne new heroes would need to emerge. And it just so happened that one was on his way.

Adam Henrique began the 2011-12 season as a rookie. But he left it with his name forever etched in history. For it was during the 2012 playoffs that Henrique's star shone brightest.

As New Jersey embarked on yet another playoff run, they found themselves facing off against the always-hungry Florida Panthers.

What a classic series it was! There were epic comebacks, crazy momentum shifts and of course, a Game 7.

And it was in the second overtime of Game 7 when Henrique showed the poise of a veteran by sniping the game-winning, series-clinching goal past Panthers' netminder, Jose Theodore.

With the win, New Jersey advanced to the second round of the Eastern Conference playoffs against the Philadelphia Flyers. And when the Devils dispatched the Flyers in five games they had secured a date with destiny, as their Conference Final opponent was none other than the Rangers.

So, 18 years after the Devils suffered one of the most heartbreaking losses in franchise history, they finally had the chance to exact their revenge. And just like they did in 1994, the Devils took a 3-2 series lead going into Game 6 in New Jersey, where they once again jumped out to an early 2-0 lead.

Only, this time, the Rangers didn't have Mark Messier to bail them out. Although Brodeur must have thought Messier was on the ice when New York erased the two-goal deficit in the second period.

Could New Jersey finally slay the dragon?

A scoreless third period soon gave way to overtime and a potential nightmare scenario of having to play Game 7 back in Madison Square Garden. This couldn't be happening! The Devils couldn't lose again!

Luckily for the Devils and their fans, there would be no need to cross back over the Hudson River -- Adam Henrique saw to that.

A mad scramble by the Devils at the start of overtime had the Rangers on their heels. But could they finish the job?

The answer: YES! THEY! COULD!

As Ilya Kovalchuk and Alexei Ponikarovsky did their best to get the puck past Henrik Lundqvist, Henrique stationed himself just to the left of the Rangers' netminder. And when the loose puck found his blade, Henrique didn't miss!

At 1:03 of overtime, Henrique secured his place in Devils lore by doing what the Devils hadn't managed to do 18 years prior -- beat the Rangers.

In the now immortal words of Mike "Doc" Emrick, "IT'S OVER!"

(Just for the fun of it, here is Doc's call, *"fed onto Kovalchuk and Kovalchuk a shot that's carefully played away by Lundqvist. Now Ponikarovsky with it. THREW ONE IN FRONT! BLOCKED THERE! SCRAMBLE FOR IT THERE! THEY POKE AWAY AT IT! Still it's loose! Poked at by Kovalchuk...THEY SCORE! HENRIQUE! IT'S OVER!)*

It was on to the Stanley Cup Final where the Devils faced off against the Los Angeles Kings. Unfortunately, New Jersey didn't have what it took to topple the Kings as Los Angeles proved to be too much to handle.

For the next five seasons that was the lasting image in the minds of Devils fans, as the team went through its longest playoff drought since it first came to New Jersey. And as the years went on, so to did more of the Devils core, including, Brodeur himself, who made a short pit stop in St. Louis before officially hanging up his skates. Even the architect of those great Devils teams, Lou Lamoriello, moved on -- first to Toronto and then to the Islanders.

But the 2017-18 season brought with it a rebirth of sorts.

For you see, every negative outcome has a silver lining. And in New Jersey's case, that silver lining was the No.1 draft pick in June of 2017 -- Nico Hischier.

With Hischier in the fold, as well as an MVP season from dynamite left-winger, Taylor Hall, the Garden Staters experienced a Cinderella season of sorts as they defied expectations and qualified for the playoffs for the first time since losing to the Kings in the 2012 Stanley Cup Final. And while they fell to the Tampa Bay Lightning in a somewhat lopsided five-game series in the opening round, it was still nice to see them back in the post-season.

If only the 2018-19 season had been as kind.

Hall was hurt most of the year and numerous players saw their numbers regress. But once again there was a silver lining. And this time, his name was Jack Hughes, a generational talent who the Devils drafted with the First overall selection in the 2019 NHL Entry Draft.

It is these moments -- and more -- that have connected Devils fans through the years. And it is through the eyes of: Larry Brooks, Steve Cangialosi, Ken Daneyko, John Dellapina, Roland Dratch, Mike "Doc" Emrick, Stan Fischler, Andrew Gross, Larry Hirsch, Matt Loughlin, Corey Masisak, Mike Morreale, Deb Placey, Glenn "Chico" Resch, Chris Ryan, Bryce Salvador, Leo Scaglione Jr. and Jim Sullivan that I bring these moments -- and others -- to life.

Buckle up and enjoy the ride down memory lane!

1 LARRY BROOKS (DEVILS FRONT OFFICE)
"JOHNNY MAC" SENDS JERSEY TO PLAYOFFS FOR 1ST TIME
(@ CHICAGO STADIUM)
APRIL 3, 1988
NJD 4, CHI 3 (OT)

BACKGROUND

"With the possible exception of broken teeth, nothing is more hockey than Larry Brooks," said *NY Post* Editor-In-Chief, Steve Lynch after learning that Larry Brooks was named the 2018 recipient of the prestigious Elmer Ferguson Award -- thus earning Brooks a spot in the NHL Hall of Fame.

It was an honor for Brooks to learn of his induction and added a well-deserved feather to his cap. After all, his career at *The NY Post* began in 1976.

But how exactly did this generational career come about? And more importantly, in a career that has been spread over parts of five -- soon to be six -- decades, what Devils games and moments does Brooks consider to be his most unforgettable?

Well, for starters, Larry Brooks grew up on Manhattan's Upper West Side as a huge New York Rangers fan. In fact, he even had season tickets (Section 419). And he continued to support the Blueshirts throughout his high school years at the Bronx High School of Science and his college years at CCNY.

However, once he completed his time at CCNY, the universe decided to throw him a curveball, or rather, a hip-check.

"I got out of school, I majored in Political Science and I was going to go to Law School," said Brooks. "And I didn't. Honestly, I was looking for a job and there was a clerk's job open at *The Post*. A friend of mine was working as a clerk. He had a job as a clerk at *The Post* and they

1

were looking for somebody else to come in and work overnights. So in late October, early November of 1975 I started working as a clerk.

"I was working overnight doing agate," continued Brooks. "At that time, reporters dictated their stories into a tape recorder. And I did a lot of transcribing. There were different jobs for a clerk on the overnight. And so I was working there for a few months, a couple of nights a week -- two, three nights a week -- as a voucher employee, part-time guy. And I had a great time. I loved it, going into work overnight and talking about sports, it was great.

"Then in the summer of '76, the Olympics were in Montreal and the (daytime) sports editor, who I'd never met before, I'd never met anyone at *The Post* who worked in the daytime, wanted me to come in and work days. We'd sent writers up there and the sports editor wanted me to come in and work days. And I remember actually telling the night guy that I didn't want to and he said, 'no, well the sports editor wants you to work days.' So I went in and I was doing rewrite.

"What would happen is, a guy up there covering would call in during the day because *The Post* at that time was a PM paper. So we had like three, four, five, six, seven additions during the day and they just kept reprinting the paper with updates during the day. So, the guys covering in Montreal would call in and somebody would be assigned then to write the story for the next edition. So, Paul Zimmerman was up there covering and it was my job to do rewrite. He would call and give the information, then you'd have to write the story and you'd have to get it up pretty quick because the additions ran basically every hour, every hour and a half.

"And I know I'm making a short story long, but I ripped off a couple of stories quickly and the sports editor said to me, right there on the spot, 'who are you and what do you want to do?' So I said, 'well, I want to cover hockey.' And he gave me the job right there to cover the Islanders in '76. So I had worked for a few months as a part time clerk and then I started covering the Islanders."

Talk about doing a complete 180. There was Brooks, a born and bred Rangers fan, covering Islanders games. But boy oh boy does the story get better -- courtesy of a few twists and turns of course.

LARRY BROOKS: "(Covering the Islanders) was my first real job. I covered the Islanders starting with the '76-'77 season. Then, in '82-'83, Colorado moved to New Jersey and Billy MacMillan was the General Manager and Coach of the Rockies -- later to become the Devils. And I knew Billy pretty well because he played for the Islanders when I covered them for a couple of years. I was always pretty friendly with

Billy. And he and I were talking when he said, 'well, why don't you come work for us? Why don't you work in our PR department?'

"I thought about it. I had been at *The Post* for six years, writing full-time and I remember thinking, 'how much more can I possibly write? I've been writing for six years.' So I interviewed with Dr. John McMullen, who was the Owner. I (also) interviewed with Max McNab, who was the Executive Vice President of Hockey.

"One of the things that really appealed to me was that, first of all it was a very small operation. It was a startup operation. I knew I was going to be somewhat involved in Hockey. But I also knew I was going to have the opportunity to actually set up the PR department and make policies that would be enforced, some of them forever." (He sure did).

"And so I went and worked for the Devils. It was great. I had a great time doing it. Billy was only there for a couple of years; he got fired early in the second season actually. But it was a small group of people who worked there. We had a great time. Lou (Lamoriello) came in 1987 and I stayed for another four years before I left. But I had a great time. I worked there for nine years. I did PR, marketing and radio color commentary for the last five years that I was there."

For the fun of it, please allow me to clarify. NHL Hall of Famer, Larry Brooks was raised in New York City as a member of the fabled "Blue Seats" at Madison Square Garden. He then got his first real job as a writer covering the Rangers' rivals, the New York Islanders. And then, to complete the unusual hat-trick, he went to work for the Rangers' cross-river rivals, the New Jersey Devils. Oh, and in case that isn't enough, when he left the Devils in 1993, to go back to *The Post*, he was assigned the task of covering the Devils before ultimately returning to his roots with the Rangers in 1996 as *The Post's* Blueshirts beat writer. Talk about a whirlwind, but I digress.

As for Devils fans, let's forget about the last part where Brooks goes back to the Rangers and focus on his career in New Jersey. During his nine-year run with the Garden Staters, Brooks held a variety of titles, but he eventually became their Vice President of Communications.

And it was during his run that the Devils experienced a moment SIX SEASONS in the making. For it was the 1987-88 season that gave the Devils their FIRST PLAYOFF BERTH in franchise history. (Please note, the six seasons does not take into account their time in Kansas City and Colorado. It also ignores their brief playoff appearance in 1977-78 as the Rockies, when they were swept in a two-game series by the Philadelphia Flyers.)

Of course, it was only fitting that a moment this special would be saved for the very end of the season. And it's no wonder that it is Larry Brooks' most unforgettable game from his time with the Devils.

MOST UNFORGETTABLE DEVILS GAME

The 1987-88 season was a crucial one for New Jersey's Devils. It had been a decade since the franchise last appeared in the playoffs -- they did so in 1977-78 as the Rockies -- and they had NEVER done so while calling the Garden State their home.

In fact, from the time the Devils began life anew in Jersey (1982-83) through the 1987-88 campaign, the team had gone through FOUR Head Coaches and THREE General Managers. That's a lot of turnover for such a young team.

However, the team's third and newest GM, Lou Lamoriello, who took over in September of 1987, proved to be the key to its turnaround.

With Lamoriello running the show the Devils' culture of losing was about to come to an abrupt end. And 50 games into the season Lou fired Head Coach Doug Carpenter, replacing him with Jim Schoenfeld.

During Schoenfeld's first 30 games, the team went from being four games under-.500 to being five games over-.500. And it was that swift turnaround that saved the Devils' season. Playing in the NHL's Patrick Division, the Devils had their work cut out for them, especially since the Patrick Division was the only division in the NHL with six teams (the other three all had five teams).

With only the top-four teams in each division qualifying for the post-season, the Devils turnabout was necessary in order to thrust them into the thick of the playoff race. And coming down the homestretch of the season, the Devils, Rangers and Penguins all wanted to claim that final playoff berth.

But, of course, only one team could prevail. And the Devils and their fans certainly wanted it to finally be their time to shine.

However, there was a problem. The Rangers and Penguins refused to go away. So, with all three teams still in the hunt heading into the final day it set-up a whole host of scenarios. And for the Devils, they were peaking at the right time, having won four in a row and 10 of their last 15 heading into the season's final day. Of course, that only meant that the Devils had kept pace with the Rangers and Penguins. Plus, both New York and Pittsburgh had the benefit of playing their season finales at home, while the Devils had to venture to Chicago for a date with the Blackhawks, who themselves were post-season bound.

4

And when the Rangers and Penguins both secured victories over their respective opponents -- bringing their points totals to 82 and 81 respectively -- the pressure was on the Devils to match their divisional rivals. Luckily, the Devils owned the tiebreaker over the Rangers and with Pittsburgh only having 81 points, a New Jersey win would put them in the playoffs!

Finally, the Devils controlled their own destiny! A win and they're in! But it's not like Chicago was just going to roll over and play dead. New Jersey was going to have to fight for every last goal -- and every last point!

And now I'll turn things over to the man who wore many hats that day, Larry Brooks.

LARRY BROOKS: "I remember everyone was pretty confident. I mean the team had played exceptionally well. Sean Burke had come from the Canadian Olympic team and I think he went 10-1 that season. Chicago wasn't a very good team at all. So I remember being very, very confident. I think everybody was very confident and then the game started and it was a tough, tough game. I could see we were nervous. Obviously the Blackhawks had nothing to lose. Darren Pang was playing goal for them and he had a spectacular game. Actually, it was funny, there was a play, I forget which Blackhawks player it was, but (the player) actually beat Burke from like 60 feet, but the play was whistled offside.

"Nobody knew it. It was kind of weird seeing Sean give up that goal, even though it didn't count. It was a shocker because Sean was Jacques Plante and Glenn Hall and Marty Brodeur, before Marty Brodeur came along. Burke, the last few weeks of the season, was spectacular. So to see him give up that kind of, to get beaten on that kind of a shot, even though it didn't count, it was an indication it was a little bit different of a night. It was a terrific game. We scored. They tied it. We fell behind, tied it. Fell behind, tied it. And then we won it.

"I was announcing, so it's not as if I was able to just get lost in my thoughts. I mean, I was nervous. It was nerve wracking. It really was. It was great doing the game. It was great watching the game. Johnny Mac was playing on a line with Patrik Sundstrom, who was really one of the best players in Devils history. (He ended up hurting his back, so he only played a few years at a peak level for the Devils.) But after he came from Vancouver he was a terrific player and actually, Mark Johnson was playing left wing on that line, so it was Johnson-Sundstrom-MacLean.

"It was a great, terrific line.

"(The next year actually, Brendan Shanahan replaced Mark Johnson on the left on that line. And the Shanahan-Sundstrom-MacLean line is probably the second best line in Devils history behind the A-Line. It was just a great, great line. I was friends with all those guys. They were young guys. They'd never done anything in the league. So it was just a real kick. I mean it was great. Shanahan actually was a scratch in that game -- it was his rookie season and it was Easter Sunday too.)

"I just remember the puck being held in at the line. Chicago tried to get it out. It was held in I think by (Joe) Cirella and I know they moved the puck around. I'm pretty sure it was Cirella who took the shot and there was a rebound and then MacLean moved in and scored. Johnny Mac was a great goal scorer, tremendous goal scorer.

"It was great. The flight home from Chicago was great. Everything about it was great. And then the ride through the playoffs that year -- beating the Islanders, beating Washington and then playing seven against Boston. It was a great ride.

"I was the color announcer doing radio that night. I don't know if there are any tapes of the broadcast that still exist, but when Johnny Mac scored, I was upstairs and I just took -- you could hear -- I took my headset off and slammed it down and went running down to the locker room, which was all the way down in Chicago, because we were at the top.

"I went down there immediately because my next job was to oversee the post-game locker room when I was there. But I mean it's clearly the most memorable game the Devils played while I was there. There were some others along that road. I mean the final few weeks of that season and playoff games that year. But certainly the final game in Chicago is still probably, after their three Cups, the game in Chicago is like the fourth most memorable game in their history or the fourth most important goal in their history is Johnny Mac's."

MOST UNFORGETTABLE DEVILS MOMENT

LARRY BROOKS: "I remember the press conference the next summer, it was the summer of '89, where Viacheslav Fetisov came over. I mean that was historic. That press conference was a big moment. I don't know that I can pick one out really. I mean the fun of it was doing the job. Being on a team was the fun part of things. There's a lot to be said for being in an organization. The highs of winning. The lows of losing. I mean it's special, it really is. It's one thing to cover games and it's one thing to cover great games. But it's another thing to be working for a team because you're so invested in everything that goes on in the season. Really the entire experience was a good one for me.

"I enjoyed working there before Lou (Lamoriello) came. Working with Lou was an education. And now we have a friendship that's lasted forever. Working for Lou might have been the most valuable experience I had. But the '87-'88 ride and the final game were the best times.

"Also, the Mickey Mouse Game was another moment. I was doing marketing and advertising that year also. I remember we tried to get Disney; I met with Disney because we tried to get Disney to sponsor a giveaway of mouse ears when they (Edmonton) came back in, but they just weren't quite ready to do it. That was one of the great early games when Edmonton came back to the Meadowlands after (Wayne) Gretzky had called the team (the Devils) a Mickey Mouse organization.

"I also remember the first game at home against the Rangers when the Devils beat them. It was the first time the two teams had played each other.

"But you know, when I was there, it wasn't a very good team. So '87-'88 was the best run they had. We lost in the first round in '90. Lost in the first round in '91. And lost in the first round in '92. So certainly '87-'88 was the highlight. But working for the organization was an experience. It's helped me in every way. Actually, it's helped me cover games because I know more about how organizations work. I had a great time and it was the right thing for me to do at that time."

2 STEVE CANGIALOSI (MSG NETWORKS)
"ADAM HENRIQUE HAS WON IT FOR NEW JERSEY IN DOUBLE OVERTIME" (@BANKATLANTIC CENTER)
APRIL 26, 2012
NJD 3, FLA 2 (2OT)

BACKGROUND

> *"That deke by Ponikarovsky...taken...shot...SCORE! ADAM HENRIQUE HAS WON IT FOR NEW JERSEY IN DOUBLE OVERTIME!"*

Most Devils fans remember exactly where they were when New Jersey downed the Florida Panthers in dramatic fashion on the night of April 26, 2012. But there was one person with the Devils who was experiencing the thrill of a lifetime and that was Steve Cangialosi.

Today, Devils fans know Cangialosi as the voice of the team's television broadcasts on MSG Networks.

But in 2012, Cangialosi was just trying to soak in everything he could, as it was the first time in his career that he would be calling every game of a Devils' playoff series.

"You have to understand the buildup of what made that series so important," explained Cangialosi. "Selfishly, it was my first playoff series calling every game. So, selfishly, that's near and dear to my heart. But the dynamic itself was very interesting. You have to understand that when the Devils went into that playoff series, it had been a considerable amount of time since they had had any post-season success."

Hold on one second. Before we get into the series itself, let's take a step back. How is it exactly that Cangialosi came to be in the role of his dreams?

"Well, that's loaded," said Cangialosi.

(Good thing we have time).

STEVE CANGIALOSI: "By the time I was 17-years-old and a freshman in college, in the fall of 1980 or 81, I knew in some form what I wanted to do for a living. I mean, I wanted to be a sports announcer. But, where it specifically would lead was a great mystery for me at that time. And the one thing I remember people telling me when I kind of expressed an interest to them that I wanted to do this for a living was, 'that's great. Are you ready to live in poverty for a good stretch of your young adult life?' And I guess, to myself, I said, 'absolutely. Why not?'

"I think my first foray into professional sports announcing, and I use this phrase very loosely -- professional sports announcing -- is when I was a sophomore in college and one of my college classmates had landed a job at Sports Phone, which, for the uninitiated was a dial-up service before the age of the Internet -- long before the age of the Internet -- before the age of all sports radio, where if you wanted a sports score at any given time of day, we were there to provide that for you.

"It was a dial-in service. You would call (212)-976-1313. And I just thought the opportunity to do sports in anyway, shape or form, when I am 19-years-old was something that I would never pass on in a million years. Basically, you needed to have the gift of rapid-fire speech. You needed to deliver 30 scores in 60 seconds -- whether it be Major League Baseball, the NFL, College Football, the NBA, National Hockey League, and at the time, the North American Soccer League, which was in existence as well. I aced the audition.

"I impressed the gentleman who conducted the interview enough to hire me. And with that I began getting reps as an announcer. Granted, it was to a finite audience who would call in for scores. And the importance of Sports Phone back then, in the early-1980s, is probably something very difficult for a person now in 2019 to comprehend, because there are a lot of people out there, whether they're simply fanatical fans or they had a monetary interest in the game who needed the score right away.

"And that was sort of my first introduction to being that person who provides sports information verbally to anybody out there who cared. And then I began to get better at it. I had the same job for the last two years in college that I had for the first two years out of college, which certainly creates for some anxious moments, 'are you ever going to move forward with this?' But Lo and Behold, I did. I don't want to bore you and give my resume here, but this is the backstory. WNEW AM was a pretty powerful AM radio station back at the time. It was 1130 on your AM dial. They played standard music. They played Sinatra. They played Tony Bennett. They played Sarah Vaughan, but they did have a sports presence.

"It was the flagship station of the Football Giants. It was the flagship station in New York of Penn State Football. And, for a time, it was the flagship station of the New York Rangers as well. So, when they launched a sports talk show back in 1987, I just thought to myself, 'look, I'm a nobody. There's no way they're going to hire me to do a sports talk show. But what can I do to in some way be part of this?' And what I did was I made them an offer. I said to them, 'I'll cover the National Hockey League for you, all three local teams and would you be interested in using me as a correspondent to cover these games for you? And if you want, I will give you three times a week or as many times as you'd like.' Quite frankly, it turned out to be three times a week, a report on the state of the National Hockey League, with an emphasis on the local teams.

"And darn, wouldn't you know it? The guy said 'yes.' And he had somebody do something similar for the NBA, as well. Well, they paid me 20 bucks a report. I was still making my close to minimum wage salary at Sports Phone. And I said, 'okay, let's just see where this goes.' And a few months in they said, 'you're doing a good job. We like your voice. Would you be interested in coming aboard? And you could be somebody who's an associate producer of the show and also come on the air and give a sportscast twice an hour.' And I said, 'are you kidding?'

"So I jumped at that and that was my first full-time job in radio.

"I didn't have the job long, because unbeknownst to me, the executive editor at WINS Radio, 1010 WINS would be listening to me on his ride home each and every night. And in that summer of 1987, sports radio had just burst onto the scene. All Sports Radio, WFAN was born in New York on a summer day in 1987. And the news stations at the time, in particular 1010 WINS, which didn't have a strong sports presence, started to think, what do we do to fend off the competition? What we need is a full-time sports anchor in the afternoon and the early evening. And after a process, I got the job.

"So, suddenly I'm 23-years-old and I'm anchoring sports radio in the biggest city in the country. So I'm thinking, 'wow, this is it. Fantastic.' It's a job I had for five years and it's a job that I loved. But I also understood at the time that there were limitations to what you were going to be able to do. So, I knew I wanted to do things more long-form. And I always knew I wanted to call games too.

"Then, I left 1010 WINS for a considerable cut in salary to go to New York One, which was a fledgling cable operation that was born on September 8th, 1992, as their primary sports anchor, at night, doing an hour long sports talk show each and every night -- without a lot of resources to do it, by the way. Basically, I'd do a couple of highlights. You'd take some phone calls, you'd do some interviews and more often than not, we were figuring out creative ways to fill an hour of sports television every night. But that also helped me greatly. To have that platform, again in New York, was very special to me.

"So I left New York One after seven years and I left without a full-time job, because I thought it had run its course. And ESPN Radio, I began to freelance a little bit for back in the late-1990s and they had gauged my interest in coming aboard to be more of a regular presence.

"Then, in 2000, I said, 'okay.' Now, while this was going on, I always knew I wanted to work at the MSG Network. While all of this was happening, I always knew that's the place I want them to be. I wanted to be at the place that was the king of regional sports anywhere. Not only in these parts, but all throughout the country. And you have to understand, at the time; MSG Network had the rights to anything and everything that was important. It had the rights to the Rangers. It had the rights to both Baseball teams, the Yankees and the Mets. It had the rights, by the time I came aboard, to all three local National Hockey League teams and they did some collegiate sports, this is where you wanted to be. And there was a big presence at night with MSG Sports Desk.

"So look, if you're a New Yorker and you're a sports fan and you want to work in sports television, at the time there was only one place you wanted to work. And the gentleman at the time who was running the network, a smart guy by the name of Mike McCarthy, just kept holding me off at bay. I just got the feeling well, 'I don't know. Is he interested at all or is he just being nice?' He would return messages, but there was never anything where, I was close to getting a job. So finally I say yes to ESPN Radio and I'm living in Connecticut at the time. So the trip up to Bristol every day is not a big deal. And sure enough, three months after I settled in there, finally, MSG Network calls me.

"That's the way life works sometimes, right?

"So now, it's like, 'oh boy, what do I do?' I had just started this new project at ESPN. I can't turn this down. This is what I was hoping for all this time. They were cool about it. They understood and I started at MSG Network as an anchor in that summer of 2000 and in one way, shape or form, I've been at MSG Network for 19 years. But here's the thing, I've been at MSG Network that long, but it's like I've had many different jobs. It feels like I've had three or four careers there, in that time, from 2000 to 2019.

"I was the weekend anchor on Sports Desk. Then for a brief time I became one of the main anchors on Sports Desk and then in 2006, came word that Matt Loughlin, in 2006 there were some changes on the landscape for the New Jersey Devils and Matt Loughlin moved to the radio side in 2006 after being a long-time host and I had some affiliation with the Devils broadcast already just being an anchor at MSG.

"What happened? I was very often that presence from the studio desk doing highlights and breaking Hockey news on the pre-game and between periods on many Devils' broadcasts. So there was some familiarity with me. And I remember that when Matt made the decision to go to radio that well this is something that I think is so much more in line with what I really want to do. I want to do live events. And of course, I want to start doing more play-by-play, which I hadn't done regularly since college at NYU. So, we actually went through the process of expressing an interest. Lou Lamoriello, of course, had to sign off on it. I think Doc Emrick and Chico Resch were also very instrumental, along with Roland Dratch, in the final decision. And I remember, I didn't know for sure that the job was mine until a couple of days before the season actually started, not camp, but the season itself.

"I remember being in the Devils' locker room two days before the season began, introducing myself to Marty Brodeur and I couldn't say with absolute clarity that I was the host of Devils Hockey that year. I thought so. But they were being a little bit evasive. And then, finally, boom, it was settled. The next thing I knew, I was on a plane to Carolina for the first Devils' broadcast that I would be part of. What I remember about that first show was how great Emrick was. And I kept thinking, we all went out in Raleigh for a very informal dinner as the crew got together for the first time. And I remember Mike personally welcoming me to the crew, saying a lot of nice things, 'we've been watching you,' all of that stuff. But the thing that stood out was that right away, I could tell he valued what I had to say. He valued my opinion, wanted to know what I thought of the team, wanted to know what I thought of the state of the league.

"And to a degree, he might've been testing me a little bit. But I think more than that, this was somebody who is an iconic broadcaster, who's very popular with the fans, whose credibility is impeccably unquestioned. And he wanted to know what I could bring to the table. And that opened my eyes; I think to what being a professional is largely about. Generally the person who asks the most questions wins. I had a nice run as Devils Host -- it went for five years.

"During that time, I think the Devils' biggest concern, there was no doubt that they were comfortable with me as a host in short order. But back then Doc was not only doing the Devils regularly, he was also juggling some assignments for NBC and everybody knew that when the calendar turned past New Year's Day, that's when my role, not only as the Host of Devils Hockey, but as Mike's backup would kick in. And I think there was some question, 'okay, what are we in for here? We're all going to find out together.'

"My first NHL broadcast for the Devils, which I'll never forget: Nassau Coliseum, January, 2007. Claude Julien is the Head Coach. And for 58-and-a-half minutes, it's quite possibly the worst hockey game you can watch. It's 0-0. Think of the classic Devils strength of locking down an opponent at the time. Giving them nothing, where one of the most valuable players on the ice for 60 minutes is a tossup between Jay Pandolfo and Sergei Brylin and you're getting the kind of game that it was. I mean, there wasn't much going on. And I remember Chico actually barking out during the broadcast, 'Cangy, it's your first NHL game and I just don't know that you're going to get to yell score tonight.' Finally, with under a minute and a half remaining, John Madden, out of nowhere, just took the loose puck and scored. The Devils had the lead.

"Hey, I just called my first NHL goal. Then with seven-tenths of a second left, Miro Satan ties it for the Islanders and we're not sure whether the goal counts until they look. Yes, it will count. And then Scott Gomez won it in overtime. So, it was this 58-and-a-half minute process of watching paint dry and then the culmination of five exhilarating minutes to cap off what was my first NHL broadcast.

"I remember that first year, I only got to fill in for Doc about five times prior to the Stanley Cup playoffs. And then I actually called the last game at the Meadowlands because Doc had an NBC commitment and I actually called that last game, which was an elimination game against the Ottawa Senators. That workload as the Number Two play-by-play guy in the Devils' television family grew each year -- Doc was getting more and more on his plate. And I remember, by the time we reached his last season with the club, I think I had called about 17 of the 82 games, where it started, minimally at five, it became more and more. And then Doc, of course, made a, I'm sure what was a very difficult decision for him to go to NBC exclusively and say goodbye to Devils fans in that summer of 2011.

"I think it was a point where I was going to be considered for the job out of familiarity with the crew, familiarity with the team, but I certainly wasn't sure that I would be the one to take the full-time mantle as the Voice of Devils Hockey on MSG Plus; well, not until I met with Lou Lamoriello personally did I realize it was actually going to happen and I'm sure that The Garden interviewed a lot of fine candidates for that job. I know they did.

"But it was pretty late in the summer. It was August 2011, when I got a phone call saying Lou wants to meet you in his office and I'm thinking it's going to be something akin to a job interview. I sit down in the office, 'hey Lou, how are you doing? How's your summer?' We got all the pleasantries out of the way and he goes, understand the dynamic here. I work for MSG Network, but the Devils have to sign off on the play-by-play and analyst job. They have to give the blessing to say, 'this is good. Go ahead, go work your contract with that particular talent.'

"And it wasn't until I sat across from Lou in his office and he said to me, he goes, 'look, I'm just here to tell you that I told MSG that we want you.' He goes, 'and it's not even a question.' I go, 'that means an extraordinary amount to me that you would invite me here just to say that.' And he goes, 'do you have any concerns at all?' And I remember I started to tell him, 'well, I don't have a concern, but I understand the challenge of succeeding a very popular play-by-play man, one of the greatest ever to do this, who's very popular with the fan base here.' And in that moment, Lamoriello was extraordinary. If he was ever extraordinary with me, it was in that moment because he cuts me short and he says to me, he goes, 'look, don't worry about succeeding the Hall of Famer. Don't worry about Chico, who's had the same partner for 16 years. Do your job. Do you understand? Do your job, the rest takes care of itself.'

"And even during the early stages of my time as play-by-play announcer, when I can tell that I wasn't the most popular guy amongst the fan base. I thought about that conversation a lot and it carried me through what I thought was the most difficult part of the transition. And I think it took awhile for Devils fans to actually embrace me as the voice of the team and make me feel the way I feel now as I'm talking to you years later."

WOW! Good thing we had time! All jokes aside though, it was Cangialosi's perseverance that led him to be in the role he's in today. And I'm sure the Devils and their fans wouldn't have it any other way.

Now, as for that series against Florida...

MOST UNFORGETTABLE DEVILS GAME

The 2011-12 season was one of both change, as well as a return to normalcy. For the Devils entered the season with a brand new Head Coach in the presence of Peter DeBoer AND they managed to return to the playoffs after having their streak of THIRTEEN CONSECUTIVE seasons making the post-season snapped the year prior (2010-11).

And don't let their fourth-place finish in the NHL's Atlantic Division fool you. These Devils were a hell of a team. They ranked 11th in the NHL in scoring and 8th in goal prevention. Of course, most of the great Devils teams have been fantastic at preventing the opposition from scoring.

Everything seemed to be in place for New Jersey to claim its fourth Stanley Cup. They had a terrific mix of veterans (headlined by Patrik Elias and Marty Brodeur), rookies (headlined by Adam Henrique) and players in their primes (headlined by Ilya Kovalchuk, Zach Parise and Andy Greene).

All they needed was a little bit of luck. And thanks to the NHL's now defunct 1-8 playoff seeding system, the Devils managed to qualify for the post-season in spite of their fourth-place finish in the division. (To be fair, they did net 102 points, which was good enough to tie them for the fourth-highest total in the Eastern Conference.)

And while there was never much doubt about whether or not they would make the playoffs, there were questions about just how far they could go in a stacked Eastern Conference. Luckily, the Devils were peaking at the right time as the entered the post-season on a six-game winning streak. (Remember, the team who is hottest and healthiest at the end is normally the one left holding the trophy).

So, as the Devils prepared to face the Panthers in the opening round of the playoffs, they knew their mission -- winning the Stanley Cup -- wouldn't be easy.

Florida was a pesky team for sure, but on paper this appeared to be a one-sided matchup in favor of the Garden Staters. There was just one problem.

As Cangialosi noted earlier, the Devils hadn't had much playoff success in the recent past. In fact, they hadn't made it past the Quarterfinals since beating Tampa Bay in the spring of 2007. Plus, the Devils were still somewhat haunted by their epic collapse against Carolina in the 2009 Quarterfinals. (Let's go ahead and erase that series from our memory banks).

Unfortunately, when the Devils opened the playoffs by dropping Games 2 and 3 to Florida to fall behind in the series 2-1, things didn't exactly look good for them. However, Coach DeBoer and the team's veteran leadership stayed the course and after a 4-0 win in Game 4 evened the series, things looked like they would begin to stabilize.

Or maybe not, as Florida returned the favor by shutting out New Jersey in Game 5 by the score of 3-0, thus putting the Devils on the brink of elimination.

However, the Devils had one thing on their side. They were headed home for Game 6. And home is exactly where the Devils wanted to be as they won 24 games at the Prudential Center during the regular season, in addition to their Game 4 win several nights earlier.

Just like clock work, the home cooking paid off as the Devils pulled even in the series with a 3-2 win in overtime -- forcing a Game 7 back in Florida.

Could the Devils conjure up enough magic to advance to the next round?

STEVE CANGIALOSI: "I think what haunted a lot of the players on that team was the playoff collapse versus Carolina in Game 7 in 2009. And there were many holdovers on that 2012 team that I think still carried the burden of choking in Game 7 with them years later.

"The epic comeback by Carolina, tying it late and winning it late and seeing a Devils second round series against the Washington Capitals get taken off the board immediately. I don't think a lot of the players, would have escaped the ghost of that series until they won another series," opined Cangialosi. "So here we are, Game 7 and the series had a lot going for it. Marty Brodeur was pulled in one of those games and didn't like it one bit, by Pete DeBoer. He came back the next start and posted a shutout against the Panthers to even up the series at two games apiece.

"But as we approached Game 7, here's what I remember about that day. I remember arriving really early for the morning skate and I mean, I got there about an hour before the players were even going to hit the ice. I remember arriving there and already in the hallway is Lou, saying good morning, pacing up and down the hall, a couple of his public relations people, including Pete Albietz, who's the Vice President of the Devils Communications today. And you have to understand, one of the things that Lou always prioritized was always making sure his players were in the best possible position to be prepared to play. And one thing he could not stand was distractions.

"So I remember saying good morning to him, shaking his hand, saying hello to one or two of the coaches and then, this is somebody that I have a very good relationship with, he kindly asked me if I could leave the area and then had his PR people kind of section off that area of the hallway until the locker room access was to begin. I've seen Lou in that situation many times and it's always with the best intention of making sure nothing distracts his team and nothing takes away from the best opportunity to win.

"I think in The Old Garden, before the renovation happened, before the bridges and before all the changes, I would in particular always see him with antenna up, because that was always an area of commotion in that center hallway. If you ever remember that Old Garden, sort of the divide between the Rangers side and the visiting team side and there always seems to be a hundred people walking around in

16

that very confined space for who knows what reason and I think that's sort of a situation where always, who is this? Why is he here? Does he need to be here? Well, this was something where his team was about to play an advance or go home game and he didn't want any distractions. So that's the first thing that I remember about that day.

"I also remember talking to Patrik Elias, who, in particular, aside from being one of the great players in the team's history, aside from being the leading score in team history, is more associated with clutch moments. (He had) 80 game winning goals in his career. Setting up (Jason) Arnott for the Cup-clincher in 2000. Scoring the game-winner in the Eastern Conference Final against the Flyers in that same year. And I remember asking him that day, 'when everyone else seems to be in awe of the moment, how do you stay so calm during a Game 7? Your best moments appear to be in Game 7's.' And I'll never forget the answer he gave me. He said, he goes, 'what I do is, I trust myself. I trust all of the work that I put in to get to this moment. And then I just play.'

"And darn it if I didn't think that that resonated throughout the entire room that morning as the Devils we're getting ready to take the ice for Game 7. There was a calmness about them, even though there was so much at stake.

"So the game begins and what everybody remembers about that night is Adam Henrique scoring in double overtime.

"But, Adam Henrique also started it for the Devils that night. He scored the first goal of that game. (He had played one game in a late-season call up the previous year. So yes, rookie status for him). So, Henrique scores and by and large it's a great start for the Devils that night. We get to the second period, Stephen Gionta scores to double the lead.

"At this point you are watching the Devils suffocate the life out of a Panthers team that you could just see was very uncomfortable at this point, on home ice, with their season on the line. And the Panthers, a team that had not won a playoff series since 1996 -- let's not forget that. So there's an immense amount of pressure.

"In that second period, Brodeur had no work at all. I think the Panthers officially had two shots on goal in that second period and you are sitting there, or at least I was sitting there calling the game and I was saying, 'this is everything that makes the Devils comfortable. There was no way that this game was ending with the Panthers putting two by Marty Brodeur to tie up this game and make any issue of who's about to win.' It's all falling the Devils' way.

"Then in the third period they score. And then, with under four minutes to play, in a 2-1 game, Marek Zidlicky puts a puck over the glass and it's a delay of game penalty. Then, moments later, power-play, Marcel Goc ties it and the place explodes. I mean it just explodes. They had tried to bring back the flavor of the plastic rats on the ice, during that whole series and now all of a sudden, in a matter of minutes, the whole dynamic has changed. Where the Florida Panthers, a team looking at the pressure now, of going a SIXTEENTH CONSECUTIVE YEAR without winning a post-season series, now it shifts to the Devils again, who might be their worst enemy now in an elimination game as they had been for several times, including 2009.

"So the first overtime happens, and in the first overtime, Marty Brodeur was extraordinary. He made 12 saves. He saved the Devils. There were goalmouth scrambles for the puck. And I remember (Tomas) Kopecky and (Kris) Versteeg saying at the end of the night that Brodeur was terrific.

"It was really dangerous doings in the crease. There were a couple of times the Panthers just couldn't get a big stick on it. Marty did not have the tremendous glove save or anything like that in that sequence. He was just really strong and in the first overtime he was very good as well.

"Then, double-overtime, a couple of minutes in, Henrique, game-winner and finally the weight is off the back of the players who waited a long time.

"You might not think a five-year drought of winning a playoff series is a very big deal, for that team in particular. But it was, because there was heartbreak and disappointment.

"Remember what proceeded it. '08, they got beat by Scott Gomez and the Rangers in five games. The Carolina collapse at the end spoke for itself. Lou Lamoriello was furious with his team's effort losing to the Flyers, who were eventually a Stanley Cup Finalist in 2010 and in 2011 they missed altogether.

"So, this team, that won three Cups in a span of eight-years, had set a benchmark for success in the Lamoriello Era. It had been, for them, five-years, could be defined as an excruciating weight to get back. And with that, the pressure was off, and then you just saw them play for the balance of the Stanley Cup playoffs. The Flyers were no match. The Rangers gave them a fight, but the Devils were clearly the better team. And finally they ran into the buzz saw in L.A. in the Final.

"So, Deb Placey and Ken Daneyko are downstairs and they are anchoring our coverage downstairs. Chico and I are upstairs in the booth having just called the game. A lot of the interaction with players and coaches happens from downstairs with our team back then.

"What I remember Chico and I focusing on was the breakthrough about what a series like this means moving forward for guys who weren't necessarily winning their first playoff series. But for the guys who were driving the bus this time.

"(Zach) Parise was on the team in 2007 that won a first round series. But again, he wasn't the guy that was driving the bus. Now, he's the captain.

"Ilya Kovalchuk's career was littered with NHL failure and suddenly here he is, he's part of this.

"And I think we looked at it as if the sleeping giant has awoken. I remember that being our approach in the playoffs, because remember the Panthers were the three-seed in the East. The Devils were the six. But I think most people had predicted the Devils would go and win that game and win that series. Most had predicted the Devils to win the series because they were the stronger team in the latter stages. And not only that, physically, they were built for it. And I remember us in our post-game conversation talking about, now that the pressure of just finally winning one is gone. Where do they go from here and can you see it mapped out where this has the makings of a long playoff run, because one thing that team did was when so many 50-50 puck battles.

"Think about the players who were on that team. Stars like Kovalchuk. But Dainius Zubrus, big and strong. Alexei Ponikarovsky, who got an assist on the Henrique double-overtime winner in the series that I'm talking about. Big and strong and would win battles. They were built for this. They were the kind of team that was really built to play into June. They just needed somebody to take care of the Kings for them before the Stanley Cup Final. Because by the time they got to the Stanley Cup Final, I thought they were almost looking at a mirror image of themselves and a team that was just a little bit hotter and had a little bit more talent."

MOST UNFORGETTABLE DEVILS MOMENT

STEVE CANGIALOSI: "(My most unforgettable moment is) Marty Brodeur on the night of 552 and the circus that was the scene on ice in the immediate aftermath of the game. The lead up to that was I got to call 551. Doc had an NBC assignment and I got to call Marty's 551st win, tying Patrick Roy for most all-time, with Roy in the house, in Montreal watching from a suite. By Brodeur standards it was just a neat, tidy 22-save victory that night and the Devils wanted so badly for him to make NHL history at home.

"So three nights later they're coming home to face the Blackhawks at The Rock and if they don't get him 552 that night, they're going on the road for the next game. If they don't beat the Blackhawks, they're going on the road to Carolina. What do you do? Hold Brodeur out? Remember, he was red-hot at that time. That night that he won in Montreal, he had won seven of his first eight since coming back from injury. And the Devils are still fighting for things that are tangible in the standings.

"If you don't beat the Blackhawks, you're going to Carolina and then you come home for one more and then you're going on the road for three. You want it to be that night against the Blackhawks. You absolutely want that to be the night, the place was packed. The anticipation in the building was tremendous. So, Doc is doing the game with Chico and I am the third member of the broadcast and the Blackhawks in the final seconds come close. There's one final save with about a second-and-a-half remaining. And then, BOOM, it's over; Brodeur's the winningest goalie of all-time!

"I'm in the Zamboni area at that point and it's my job as soon as the glass opens to bust out on the ice. And I know that my responsibilities are to interview the star of the game on the ice before the entire live house. But who knows how this is going to play out now because NHL history has just been made. It's bedlam. And I remember the scene; Brodeur is being congratulated by all of his teammates.

"They're mobbing him and somebody says here are scissors cut the net and Brodeur starts to cut the net. It's pretty hard to cut the twine of an NHL official goal. Who knows what kind of scissors he was handed at the last moment. You could tell he's laboring and Jamie Langenbrunner just skates over to him, shaking his head. He goes, 'give me that.' He goes, 'go take a victory lap or something.' And Brodeur actually wound up taking the victory lap around the ice and the scene of him trying to cut the net, all of a sudden being told, 'get outta here Big Boy. Go celebrate with the fans,' and his teammate taking over for him and me standing there, I'm thinking, 'this is a pretty cool job.'"

3 KEN DANEYKO (NJ DEVILS & MSG NETWORKS)
"JOHNNY MAC" OT GWG NETS DEVS 1ST PLAYOFF BERTH
(@CHICAGO STADIUM)
&
"IT'S OVER!" NEW JERSEY VANQUISHES THE GHOSTS OF 1994
(@PRUDENTIAL CENTER)
APRIL 3, 1988 & MAY 25, 2012
NJD 4, CHI 3 (OT) & NJD 3, NYR 2 (OT)

BACKGROUND

When you think about a list of the most beloved Devils players of All-Time, there are quite a few names that come to mind: Martin Brodeur, Scott Niedermayer, Scott Stevens and Patrik Elias to name several.

But there is another name that is always part of the conversation as well and that's Ken Daneyko.

From the time Daneyko debuted during the 1983-84 season, until he hung up his skates following the Devils' Game 7 triumph in the 2003 Stanley Cup Final against the Mighty Ducks of Anaheim, you would not find a tougher, grittier defensemen in a New Jersey sweater.

Oh sure, Niedermayer and Stevens got most of the attention of the Devils' blue line, largely due to their outstanding offensive numbers, but it was Daneyko who brought that added dimension of toughness to the Dev's backend.

And not long after "Dano" retired he found himself making the transition from player to broadcaster -- a job he's held since 2006. And it is his broadcaster's acumen that has allowed Daneyko to connect with a new generation of Devils fans, thus allowing him to continue to garner affection from New Jersey's devoted fan base.

But how did Ken Daneyko get to become such a heart and soul piece of the Devils franchise?

KEN DANEYKO: "I mean, where I grew up in Western Canada, near Edmonton, obviously, the Edmonton Oilers, who had been in the WHA as the Alberta Oilers when I was a kid, were a big influence as far as in the area. And when I was a kid, they became the Edmonton Oilers. But, by that time, I was 16 years old when they entered the National Hockey League. It was what I wanted to do. Hockey was a religion in Canada, no different than hundreds, thousands of kids in Canada. We all wanted to be hockey players."

From growing up in a Hockey crazed country to playing in parts of three decades and hoisting three Stanley Cups to boot, Ken Daneyko certainly lived out his dream of being a professional hockey player. And his playing days were over, he knew he wanted to stick around in some capacity. Little did he know that it would lead to a second career as a broadcaster. And that second career is still going strong to this day.

KEN DANEYKO: "I don't know if that's really what I wanted to become. I wasn't 100% on that. I just wanted to stay in the game in some capacity. I'd done some stuff for a little bit the last couple of years of my career on radio and been on some shows along the way, not just hockey but some sports stuff. I kind of fell into it.

"Ed Coleman was a good friend and I did some stuff with him on Saturday nights because I was a sports junkie and was really into it. He'd always bring me on and would even do baseball; I was a big baseball guy. So I got on there a little bit, off and on. And I'd felt that people would tell me during my career and near the end of it, even reporters, that I'd always been a very open guy, a guy who spoke well as far as giving answers to reporters. And there were questions of, 'are you thinking of broadcasting after your career is over?' And I said, 'oh, I don't know.' I wasn't really thinking about it, but possibly. I knew I wanted to stay with the Devils in some capacity. And besides being in the community, I knew that that was a possibility. I was going to get an opportunity strictly from the standpoint that I'd been there a long time and I knew I would probably get that chance if it interested me.

"MSG, and obviously a lot of people have changed over the years, but was it SportsChannel at the time? I don't know specifically the person (who brought me on board) because it's been different people. I started doing stuff right after my career; I think it was Roland Dratch (Devils Producer) maybe to tell you the truth. It wasn't really a job yet. I was just coming on with Stan (Fischler) every once in a while. I did a couple of things, not officially really working, just kind of doing some stuff in between periods as well as post-games.

"Then in 2006, was kind of when I officially started. I think SportsChannel had been taken over by MSG, I don't know the timeline there, but at MSG there were different people there who hired me and asked me to do pre-game, post-game and in-between periods -- mostly the home games. I said, 'sure, it sounds good because it was the Devils.' And obviously the Devils thought it was good too. Lou Lamoriello always thought that'd be a good area for me if I were interested. But Roland Dratch was a big influence too. We were close when I was a player. He was always a great guy and he's been doing it for a long time, as far as producing. So that was kind of how it all got going. And then the rest really is history.

"It's been a lot of Devils stuff, as well as the Hockey Show which we did for eight years with Butch Goring, Don Maloney, Stan Fischler and Al Trautwig. It was a great learning experience for me. I learned a lot from all of those guys, especially Al. He's an iconic guy. And he was always picking up little things when I'd ask. It was just a little advice here and there. And he always used to say, 'be yourself,' things like that. It was good to do this. We also did a Hockey Night Live. We did it out of The Garden from a small, little room for about a year or two, like a little dungeon. We thought it was going to last three months and it ended up lasting three years -- every Saturday night. So that was a lot of fun and got things going. But obviously, I was doing my Devils stuff too. That show really helped nurture me along the way."

MOST UNFORGETTABLE DEVILS GAMES

It was the spring of 1988 and the New Jersey Devils were still searching.

What were they searching for?

The answer: a way to gain entrance to the Stanley Cup playoffs.

Ever since touching down in New Jersey in 1982 -- they were officially christened, The Devils, on June 30, 1982 -- the team had not experienced much, if any, success. Oh sure, there were some small highlights, like the team hosting the annual NHL All-Star Game during the middle of the 1983-84 season. But by and large the team's move from Colorado to New Jersey was not a success.

That is, until Lou Lamoriello took the reigns as General Manager in the fall of 1987. With "Sweet Lou" calling the shots the Devils began to change the perception that they were failures. And one of the first big moves that Lamoriello made was to fire Head Coach Doug Carpenter 50 games into the 1987-88 season.

And while history isn't normally on the side of teams who fire their coach so deep into the season, this time it worked out, for the Garden Staters brought in Jim Schoenfeld to man the bench. And under Schoenfeld the team turned itself around, thus saving its' season.

From toting an under-.500 record after 50 games, to playing over-.500 during the final 30, New Jersey was in the midst of a Cinderella type run. And that run was not complete without a trip to the Eastern Conference Final.

However, the Devils don't make it nearly that far if it wasn't for the heroics of their terrific right-winger, John "Mac" MacLean.

With the Devils eyeing their first ever trip to the playoffs, they needed everything to break just right heading down the homestretch. And break right it did as the team won 10 of 15 games heading into the season's final day. But things also broke right for the Rangers and Penguins, who were right on the Devils' heels.

Luckily, New Jersey controlled its own destiny. A win and they were in!

So, five years into his career, could Ken Daneyko help his team take the next step and advance to the post-season?

KEN DANEYKO: "It was the game that really turned the franchise around. You could see the excitement of our young group.

"We were nervous as can be. Excited, nervous, crazy. It was all about making the playoffs. In our existence, since things started in '82 -- I was drafted that year. Johnny Mac was the following year. Kirk Muller the following year after that -- I mean (Brendan) Shanahan was there as an 18-year-old. Joe Cirella was on the team. We were just all a very tight knit group, all a bunch of young guys trying to live a dream. And just getting in the playoffs first, I mean anybody that saw it, we celebrated like we won the Stanley Cup.

"It was, we didn't know what to do with ourselves. But just all the nerves and excitement -- we had played the night before at home. So we were exhausted and on a 7-0-1 tear. But we went strictly on adrenaline. I think the night before we had beat the Islanders, if I'm not mistaken. And we needed every single last point just to get in. And we ended up knocking out the Rangers who ended up not making it because they, had won a game, I believe it in the afternoon to be up on us a couple points, but we ended up winning with a tiebreaker -- something like that. But yeah, it was pandemonium. Just crazy and as excited as I've been because we didn't really know how to respond and we're all kids only had been in the league a few years. A lot of our guys, sprinkled in with veterans obviously, but we learned how to celebrate better when we won Cups and were better.

"It was great. We were nervous, couldn't have been any more nervous. I scored the opening goal. Oh, it was crazy. Obviously, we had a lot of nerves being the young group and Kirk Muller made an unbelievable move through the neutral zone. He gained the blue line and one-handed a puck around a defenseman then spun it back and I came into the play just inside the blue line. He made an unbelievable play and set it up on a tee. I took the slap shot and got all of it and we went up 1-0.

"Then I had to go to the bench to change. Jim Schoenfeld, the coach at the time, said, 'stay out there.' I hadn't been out there long and I said, 'I can't. I'm too excited. I gotta settle down here for a second.' So he changed the D-pair just cause I told them I was too excited. I needed to regroup a little bit because the game was so important to us all.

"Then, in overtime, I was on the ice. I had a great opportunity (in overtime) myself. I was with Joe Cirella on the ice, so it was, I just remember it and it was like slow motion.

"Joe Cirella had it inside the blue line, took a quick little snapshot from the right side and the puck caromed right out to Johnny (Mac) in the high slot. I was probably five, six feet behind him really. He was more on the left side and the right-handed shot in the high slot and I was the left, so I could see him perfectly at his point because he got to the rebound.

"It came right out, kicked right out to him after the Cirella shot and I was right behind Mac. I could kind of see the puck going in -- I can't remember now if it was far side, but all I cared about was that it was in. I had a pretty good vantage point and the rest is history. But at that point it was pandemonium. We were like kids in a candy store. We went nuts and it was pretty exciting. And obviously we were able to carry that excitement during the playoffs and win a couple of rounds."

As exciting as that game was for a young Ken Daneyko, he also had the opportunity to be a part of a couple unforgettable Devils game as a broadcaster.

KEN DANEYKO: "Well, I wasn't doing the color, but I was doing the in-between periods and pre-game, or pre-game and post-games. And I'd have to say the ones that stand out to me are the (Adam) Henrique Game 6 against the Rangers -- the 'Henrique, It's Over!' call by Doc (Emrick). That's one that really stands out to me. I also have to go with the Florida Game 7 comeback in the first round that same year -- the year they went to the Stanley Cup in 2012. Those games, just the excitement, you know, I'm emotionally invested, I've been there forever as a player and with the organization and just so happy for the guys, in both those series, in the way they won them in dramatic fashion --

Henrique twice, against the Florida Panthers and against the Rangers in overtime.

"It's all about winning to me.

"It was pandemonium. Obviously, you beat your archrival. I played in so many of those rivalry-type series against the Rangers and lost some along the way. We had some epic series, but the excitement of a rivalry and it was a terrific series. It was just like some of the ones I was in against them in '94 when we lost. It was just an epic series when we looked back. And that's the same as 2012. When you're not playing you're having the same feeling as the fans. You kind of get to see it through the fan's eyes because you are a fan as well, even though you are calling the game or breaking down the game as an analyst; whatever it may be.

"But good, bad, indifferent, you've gotta give your honest assessment. But on the flip side of it, I was rooting for them like a fan. Just to feel their excitement and especially as it's so nerve wracking, way more so than a player's. You can't do anything about it. That whole run was just phenomenal, in 2012, in those overtime games. I just remember the first round when (Travis) Zajac scored in Game 6 in overtime and then game 7 (with Henrique). Then, fast-forward a couple of series later against the Rangers it was pretty incredible. Unfortunately, we fell short as far as winning it all. But those are just amazing feelings.

"I was in Florida for the double-overtime Game 7. And I told Roland Dratch on the mic, I was in the room, I kept running. I was so nervous. I was a mess. If I'm recalling it correctly, Florida came back and tied it at 2. I already thought the game is over, the Devils were gonna win it. And Florida, I think, scored relatively late in the third to tie it, if I'm not mistaken. I was just devastated. And I told Roland on the mic, on the headset, 'I can't go on if they lose.' And I said, 'I can't. I won't, I can't.' Then he goes, 'you've got to.' I was like, 'no, screw it. 'I'm bad. I'm emotionally invested. I said, 'I'll be super pissed off.' Thankfully they won and we can laugh about it now. He'd never seen anybody like that. I was having a heart attack and I was running in and out, watching a little bit of the overtime, running back to the studio. And I was by the Devils; dressing room, on ice level, when they won. I was going crazy, that's for sure.

"(As for the Rangers Game 6), I was just like in Florida. I go crazy during those. I wear my emotions on my sleeve. And I'm a lot more nervous than I ever was as a player. I'm just rooting for their success. And like I said, being emotionally invested as I am, it was hard to watch. Let's put it that way. Very hard to watch. But the good news was, they had one more opportunity (should they have lost Game 6), although you don't want to go back to The Garden for Game 7. I know anything can happen in Game 7, but obviously it was going to be more difficult.

"Those (games) were exciting as broadcasters and being part of the team as far as covering them, calling them. You're emotionally invested all year, all of us. Everybody handles it differently. I was probably more nervous than everybody cause that's just my personality. But we all were, I remember Deb (Placey) rooting and all and we were all really excited. It was tough to watch it. It was gut wrenching. You're sitting on every play, every opportunity on both teams and Deb's probably right, I might've thrown up if we had lost."

MOST UNFORGETTABLE DEVILS MOMENT

KEN DANEYKO: "There's been quite a few. But I think, my last game, Game 7 in 2003 with The Cup over my head, big Grizzly Adams' gray beard. I was getting older and getting into Game 7, it's pretty memorable to me. It was my last game, what a way to go out! It was a storybook ending for me. I was winding down and getting older. It was a scary looking picture.

"After the series I had thought I was going to play another year, for the most part. I had already discussed it with Lou (Lamoriello) and we were going to talk about me playing one more year. Back in December, January, around there -- I was already 39 -- I was getting up there. But I believed I could play one more year and then you'll see how your role goes. But things change. I was in and out of the lineup in the playoffs. I mean it was fine, it happens to a lot of players, but I still thought I could play one more year.

"Then, after Game 7, I knew right away. I wanted to go on top and had nothing left. I knew at the time I was going to be able to have the opportunity to stay in the organization, possibly by broadcasting. And I met with Lou a week later and just saw what he wanted to do. I know he wanted to implement some younger guys. Honestly, he was giving me respect and I was probably telling him what he wanted to hear when I said 'I'm done.' Then he said, 'obviously whatever you want, you'll be in the organization in some capacity' and that made me happy.

"I was a little surprised (to get into Game 7. I'd sat out the first six games of The Final). I knew before the game I was going to play and that I was pretty sure it was going to be my last game. So I just wanted to win. It was all about winning.

"I had played a long time and I knew young guys were pushing now. So I just wanted to absorb it, take it all in and just make sure I was prepared from an execution standpoint. I wasn't gonna play a ton, but I just knew every shift was important. That's it. Make sure I play sound and don't make a mistake because it would've killed me to go out and make a mistake. But you can't think like that, because if you do, you usually do. So it all worked out and the team played very well. Marty (Brodeur) was great and we won 3-0."

HASEK OUTDUELS BRODEUR IN 4-OT CLASSIC (@BUFFALO
MEMORIAL AUDITORIUM)
APRIL 27, 1994
NJD 0, BUF 1 (4OT)

BACKGROUND

When you take a look back through the history of the New Jersey Devils you will find several unofficial Era's.

First you have 1982 to 1987. The team wasn't all that good and many questioned whether they would ever turn things around.

Then you had the beginning of their rise to glory, which so happened to coincide with the arrival of Lou Lamoriello as the team's General Manager in the fall of 1987. This Era lasted until the NHL's lockout at the start of the 1994-95 season.

And just like how the lockout disrupted the ebb and flow of the NHL's regular season, so too did the Devils once peace had been made. From 1995 through to the NHL's next lockout (this time in 2004-05) the Devils were one of the preeminent teams in the League; capturing three Stanley Cups -- '95, '00 & '03 -- and were considered to be a quasi-dynasty.

The Era that began when the 2004-05 lockout concluded, (the League and the Player's Association did not come to terms until the 2005-06 season), saw New Jersey take a step back, but not a drastic one. The Garden Staters were still a perennial playoff team, they just couldn't capture a fourth Cup.

That Era ended when, ironically enough, the NHL again went through a lockout (this time a much shorter one) that delayed the start of the 2012-13 campaign. From 2013 to 2018 the Devils were not a playoff team -- their stars all either left for greener pastures or retired.

But a new Era began when New Jersey returned to the post-season in the spring of 2018. Yes they were felled in the first round. And yes they failed to return to the playoffs in 2019. But that failure allowed the team to secure the No. 1 overall draft pick in the June 2019 NHL Entry Draft. And with that pick they selected generational talent, Jack Hughes, who will hopefully preside over a new Era of Devils domination.

However, I'm getting ahead of myself. So let's return to the Era that spanned from 1987-1995. For it was this Era that saw the Devils begin to develop an identity that has remained with the team for more than two decades.

And one beat writer in particular was there to bear witness to New Jersey's transformation. His name? John Dellapina of the *NY Daily News*. (After leaving *the Daily News*, Dellapina eventually made his way to the NHL League Office, where he currently serves as the Senior Vice President of Communications).

But how and why did Dellapina come to cover the Devils during this particular span of time?

JOHN DELLAPINA: "The short story is, I didn't make the baseball team at Penn my sophomore year. Not that I should have. I couldn't hit at all. I could field, but I couldn't hit. So, then I went to *the Daily Pennsylvania* and joined the newspaper. And it was like love at first sight. It was, 'this is obviously what I should be doing with my life.' And I didn't know it until then.

"In retrospect, it all made perfect sense. I was gigantic sports fan. My dad, one of the most literate people I ever knew, brought home five newspapers a day. I can just remember lying on the floor of my kitchen and that story, reading *the Daily News*. So, the fact that I ultimately worked at *the Daily News* was, it kind of made sense in retrospect. But I went from, when I was in school; I worked at *the Philadelphia Daily News* as basically a scoreboard clerk type thing, an active clerk.

"The school newspaper was front and center there. It was a phenomenal paper. It was better than a lot of professional newspapers and it had been a sports writer factory. Some of the great, great writers, a lot of names you would know, went to Penn and worked at *the Daily Pennsylvania*. So, it was always in my face. It was always something that I had thought about. But, after I realized I could not hit a 95 mph fastball, or any kind of curve ball, I was like, 'okay, let me go there and see how that works.'

"And then I went to York, Pennsylvania, started at a tiny paper and got bigger and bigger and bigger until I finally got to *the New York Daily News*; the paper I read growing up. I always loved hockey, played roller hockey growing up in that story. And when I got a chance to cover it full-time, I didn't want to cover anything else. There were times when they offered me other beats, baseball in particular. And while I knew there was more prestige in covering baseball, I didn't want to cover anything but hockey. Just the best people in the world, the best game in the world. And so that was it. I was hooked."

MOST UNFORGETTABLE DEVILS GAME

When the 1993-94 season rolled around, the Devils had the look of a team on a mission. It was no longer enough to make the playoffs. They needed to win the Stanley Cup in order to validate themselves as an elite team. But first things first, they needed a new coach. And who better than Jacques Lemaire?!

JOHN DELLAPINA: "My first year on the Devils beat was '88-'89. I covered some of those '88 playoffs. I remember Yellow Sunday and all that. And, ironically, I now work for one of the people who was on the ground for the NHL then Gary Meagher. But anyway, by 1993-94, I had covered Jim Schoenfeld, Tom McVie, Herb Brooks, who is one of the people, when it all ends, that I'll be able to say it'll have been a privilege to have known Herb Brooks. And then Jacques Lemaire came in. I remember the summertime press conference; he walked in, a typical Lou Lamoriello production. Nobody knew who it was until the minute he walked in the door. There were no leaks. And when he walked in the door, there was an audible gasp, like, 'oh my God, they got Jacques Lemaire to coach the Devils.

"And from the first game that season, I'm trying to remember, I'd have to go back through my records. I think it was a game against St Louis," (it was actually against Tampa Bay). "But they played really well on opening night and it was an instant buy-in. In retrospect, now, everybody thinks of that Devils team as a team of automatons who just executed Jacques Lemaire's trapping system. And, you look at that roster, there was a lot of talent on that roster -- a lot of offensive talent, a lot of creative people, a lot of interesting personalities and they needed to have instant success to buy into what he wanted to do, which was sacrifice for the greater good and be structurally sound. And it happened right away.

"They got off to a crazy start, like 6-0-1 or something like that." (They started off 8-1-0). "So you have people like Stephane Richer buying into it and Claude Lemieux buying into it. And a young Scott Niedermayer, who was a phenomenal offensive talent. But this was the way you were going to play the game and they all played it that way.

31

"But I think the other thing about that season (1993-1994) and if you watch those games, the Devils in later years, under Lemaire, became a much more shut down, not that entertaining kind of team to watch. That year's Devils team was really entertaining. They scored a lot of goals. They scored on counterattacks, but they scored a lot of goals. And so when they were springing traps back then, it wasn't what people now remember as the 'Dead Puck Era.' It wasn't like the Florida Panthers teams that kind of stood still in the neutral zone and grabbed you as you went by.

"This was, they were springing traps on people and going 100 mph in the opposite direction. And then of course there was, the fourth line, the Crash Line, which was, they weren't playing a passive trap. They were beating the tar out of you behind your own net. They were an entertaining team to cover, from the guys in the locker room, from Jacques, who was just; it was like learning the game every day. Talking to him and Larry Robinson, it was a phenomenal team to cover and a phenomenal year. And there was only one team better in the NHL than the Devils that year. And it was the Rangers. And it was by a nose every single step of the way, including all six games in the regular season, which the Rangers won."

And, of course, under Lemaire, the Devils were going to do things their own way. The Rangers may have been a high-flying team, but the Devils were the soundest defensive team in the league -- with some offensive punch to boot.

JOHN DELLAPINA: "They are all different ways of playing the game, right? So there were teams back then who would dump and chase. And their idea of dump was, there were some teams like Chicago, I'll never forget in Chicago Stadium, the first five minutes of the game the puck was irrelevant. It would go into the corner, small building, pound, pound, pound and they would just hit your defensemen so often that the question was, do you want to play this game the rest of the night? Do you want to keep going back for these pucks? And then they would have an advantage. And then there were teams that just went end-to--end.

"There were teams that matched lines. Roger Neilson with the Rangers was great for that. There were teams that shadowed people. So there were different ways of playing. But this way, which was kind of a rip-off on the way that the Canadiens had played back in the day, but they were so talented that people didn't focus on that. They just focused on the 'Flying Frenchman.' It was just a structured system where each guy had a specific role and a place to play and you were disciplined then. You didn't run out of position. So, if the other team had a controlled breakout, the defensemen stopped behind the net, you weren't chasing him back there, you were never doing that and the Devils never did. If you were the left-winger, you weren't in the right offensive corner chasing that puck. Things like that didn't happen.

"They were just structured. We can get as technical as you want, 1-2-2, that's basically what the formation was. They steered you in a certain direction coming out of your zone and then the two forwards on that side would squeeze you and pinch you and trap you like a Basketball trap. And everybody else was in there supporting position. So they never, they rarely gave up odd man breaks. They were just ridiculously structured and in their own zone they had a way of playing. Larry Robinson taught stick on puck. It was just structured. It really was. And it was based on a counter attack."

And let's not forget, there was more to the Devils' stifling system than just sound defensive structure. They also had an up and coming goalie who was on the precipice of breaking out. His name? Martin Brodeur.

JOHN DELLAPINA: "I think by midway through the season, you know he's the future. Whether he's the present was still a question because, to jump ahead of series, they go play Boston the next round and (Chris) Terreri plays all the games in Boston Garden, because he was good in Boston Garden and Jacques Lemaire was that kind of coach. He was like, 'this guy's better in Boston Garden. I'm going to play him. I don't care who my Number One goalie is.' So they split a lot of the time that year. It was clear that, Chris would say, Chris knew he was grooming this kid. Chris had no illusions about that. But Marty at that point was just a wide-eyed, 'I'll do whatever you want. I'll fill the water bottles.' And it was one of the best things about Marty, even until the end of his career. He was really just a down to earth, good guy, who was one of the greatest goaltenders in the history of the world."

So, between Jacques Lemaire's structure, the Devils obvious talent on both offense and defense and the emergence of Brodeur, New Jersey seemed well on its way to getting over the hump. And when they qualified for the playoffs with a whopping 106 points, it looked like they were positioned to do just that.

However, two teams stood in their way. One was the Rangers. And given the Blueshirts' 6-0 record against the Devils in the regular season you could understand why they were an obstacle. But the other team was a bit more of a surprise.

The Buffalo Sabres were a good team during the 1993-94 season. They even tallied 95 points. But could they really be a match for the Devils?

The answer was a surprising, yes.

JOHN DELLAPINA: "The sense was that they (the Devils) had finally established their supremacy in the series, because the first four games, I think, I just read through a lot of material and I remember it now, the two games in Buffalo -- Games 3 & 4 -- the Sabers out played them pretty much for six periods. Brodeur stole a game and then the Sabres handily won Game 4. So, Game 5, the Devils finally seem to take over. The whole Rangers thing is right there because the Rangers have already swept the Islanders in a series that barely lasted four games in the first round. And so, they need to move. The Devils aren't thinking just so much, 'we have to advance past round one.' They're thinking about 'how can we get past the Rangers, ultimately?' And so, going seven games in the first round while the Rangers are going an easy four is not the way to do it.

"I remember at the time, the Rangers were resting and there was this sense that they were destined to meet each other. But this game kind of threw destiny on its' ear. But going into that game I definitely thought, 'okay, the Devils are now gonna win and we're going to go on with the natural order of things and the two best teams are going to get to each other.

"The fact was, if you were a Devil, especially in 1994, you were measured against the Rangers. Everything was measured against the Rangers. Your attendance was measured against the Rangers. Your newspaper coverage. Your television. This was the order of things. The Rangers were the big boys from Broadway and we were the guys from the suburbs and we had to get over that hump. And so that's always there. But there was no way a Jacques Lemaire coached team was thinking ahead in the sense that they're distracted. That's not the case. It's motivation. It's drive. It's not like they overlooked the Buffalo Sabres in any way and through five games, if they had thought they were gonna overlook the Buffalo Sabers, they were not by that point.

"I was thinking that it's going to end (with Game 6). The Devils' power-play had really started clicking. Hasek was a ridiculous obstacle, there's no question about it. But, by that point, the Devils just looked like they were the better team, the team that had 11 more points in the regular season, they were just a better team; better throughout the lineup, better structure. I thought the Devils; it was time for the series to end.

"I mean the night is, as you can imagine, a bit of a blur. But, the reason I picked this as the greatest Devils game I ever saw, my perspective on this is, I covered the Easter Epic. So I saw these two, four overtime games. And the Easter Epic was half of this game. The Easter Epic was, guys would play for three minutes of overtime and then hold onto each other like exhausted heavyweights just to get to the next intermission. This game was end-to-end, hammer and tongs for seven periods. It was unbelievable how these two teams went at each other. It's the totality of it.

"So, there are a lot of fun things that are just inside writer things that go on at times like this. So the 'Aud,' what a place, right? In an old barn. I mean I just remember these filthy hanging baffles that were from the roof to collect sound and they had never been cleaned. So it was just dirt hanging from the roof. And back in those days we weren't sending stories on laptops and phones. We had these TRS 80 machines and we had to plug them into phones and there was really like one phone for every two or three writers. So there was kind of like jockeying for position, who had their stories ready first. Who could plug the phone in first. You didn't unplug a phone while somebody else was filing a story. But if I'm next to the guy from the *New York Post* and I'm with the *Daily News*, I'm in no hurry to give him the phone.

"There was a little gamesmanship going on up there. So, you're filing a running (story) after the second period, which is just basically the stuff that happened in the first two periods, including the first of several waved off goals in this game. And then, after every period, you're filing more. I must've sent second period, third period, four, five and six. I must have filed five or six times that night. And you just keep updating and reordering what was important in the game. What happened in the third overtime suddenly is more important than what happened at the end of regulation. And you're just wondering what the people back in New York are doing with the stuff that you're sending, because, by now, you've sent miles and miles of copy and you're wondering if they're updating it properly. So every overtime period you're trying to come up with new ways to express the insanity that's going on.

"And after a certain point, I'm sad to say, there were no more deadlines -- I was now a fan watching the game. And I think that happened at the end of the third overtime. The Easter Epic, I made the next day's paper. I wasn't at *the Daily News* then. The paper I was working for had a later deadline and I was able to get in the paper the next day. For this, if you look on the next day's *New York Daily News* in the archives, there's no game story. And I don't know how many papers actually had a game story.

"At that point, you just want it to last all night. You know you're watching something historic. I'm young. I can stay up all night. I'm fine. Let's go; let's set a record. Mud Bruneteau, that went six overtimes, let's go six. And the way Hasek was playing, it seemed possible. Brodeur had a great game, but it wasn't nearly what Hasek had. Hasek stopped 70 shots and like 45 of them were point blank. It was unbelievable how many great chances the Devils had in that game. In contrast, the Sabres put two or three pucks past Marty, some were illegal. I mean, Wayne Presley kicked one in. There was an interference that had to be waved off. The refs either waived off or were overruled three times on goals that supposedly went in the Devils' net or they thought went in the Devil's net. So there was a lot of chaos in that game. And at that point, you're thinking, 'this seriously could go on all night.'

"It's funny. I think, in retrospect, you put import to things that don't really have any import at the time, but when you look back, so Valeri Zelepukin is standing in the slot. Now, I don't know why he's standing in the slot, he's a winger. I'm sure that's not really the Devils defensive coverage right there. Tommy Albelin's there too, the defenseman, and Jason Dawe centers the puck and it hits off Zelepukin's skate and pops into the higher slot. If it doesn't hit his skate it goes right through to safety and we play seven more overtimes. Zelepukin is the guy who later scores the goal with 7.7 seconds left to tie Game 7 of the Rangers-Devils series. So these things all seem to come together. And the goal was not, in a lot of ways, not like the Matteau goal, but in other ways it was. Marty is almost helplessly out of position at this point.

"He was reacting to a puck going from his left to his right. He's pushing hard to his right and the puck deflects into the high slot. He's now played seven periods with goalie equipment on that was a lot heavier in 1994 than it is today. He's got to get his body back across -- he had no chance. As long as Dave Hannan hit the net with a little bit of lift on the puck it was going to go in the net. He (Brodeur) tried his best to get there, but he couldn't. It's really crazy. Jacques Lemaire, in the immediate aftermath of the game said, 'that one guy blew his coverage on that and that's why the goal was scored.' He later softened that. I don't know whom he was blaming, but, fourth overtime, I don't know how anybody's to blame for anything. But anyway, your thoughts are: A) how do I get to this locker room in this unbelievable building, because I have to get through the entire crowd, cause there are no elevators in this building.

"There were escalators that go nowhere. It's a logistical, 'how do I get down there?' It's, I know I've just witnessed something historic. And again, there's a sense of how lucky can you be? I was actually at the Easter Epic game too. There's a, 'Oh my God, what time is my flight back to New Jersey?' 'I think I have to get up in two hours.' There's a lot of that going on in your head. But when you're working, you're on autopilot at a time like that. You try to put things in perspective and you do when you write, but you're just like, 'what's next?' Get to the locker room, 'who am I going to talk to?' That sort of thing.

"One of the reasons I picked this as my favorite game is that locker room scene. So, the visiting locker room at the 'Aud' was a truly disgusting place, not unlike the old Sky Rink locker room where I used to shower when I played pickup hockey. I got in there and there must've been an inch of water on the floor of the locker room because the showers had just overflowed. It was like walking into a mash unit. I mean, players were just sprawled everywhere, lying down, could barely look up. It was like, carnage is too strong a word, but it was devastation. It was physical devastation and exhaustion. It wasn't, I don't think any of them had put in perspective by then, 'oh my God, this great season could end in two days and how are we going to pick ourselves back up?'

"There was some appreciation in that room. And I read back on the quotes, that they had just been part of something unbelievable. And there was no hesitation about giving Hasek credit for one of the greatest individual performances they had ever seen. They knew they did everything they could do to win that game, 70 shots on goal. And most of them were good shots. Stephane Richer had nine of them. This is a guy who scored 50 goals in the NHL. Bobby Holik had eight. Now, he wasn't a great finisher. And the thing I remember about that room is, amid this devastation and exhaustion, was Bobby Holik, who was fresh as a daisy, bouncing around the room. And I looked at, I remember the quotes in my head, but I looked them up and he was like, 'this was my favorite thing of all time. I felt like I was getting stronger as the game was going on. I wish it had lasted all night.'

"And you have to know Bobby. I could have done an impersonation of his high-pitched voice, but he was, the guy was a physical freak. He was ready to keep playing. And I do remember and if you watch the game, as the overtimes went on, Holik became the most dangerous player on the ice for the Devils because he seemingly never got tired. He just got stronger and stronger. It was delirium quotes. Ken Daneyko said, 'we had 63,000 chances.' And that's the kind of thing Ken Daneyko would say. But those are the kinds of things you say when you're completely out of it.

"The other reason why I picked this game is because of how they responded to it. And I think that really is the story of that team and the team of that Era is how they responded to devastating defeats. I don't know if it was Lemaire, if it was Scott Stevens, if it was Lou, if it was the culture that they had already established there. But they just pressed on. There was no, 'woe is me.' There was no, 'that was our chance.' They never thought that way. We all did and we'd ask them those questions, like, 'don't you think, how many times can you cheat death?' 'Shouldn't you have gotten rid of this team earlier in the series. You don't play well early. Now you lose in four overtimes, how do you come back?'

"'Well, they're going to drop the puck in two days and we're going to just play.' And that's what they did. And that's the exact same thing they did after the devastating overtime losses in the Rangers series a month later. It's the same thing they did after losing the Matteau game and coming back the next year and winning the Stanley Cup. I mean, Martin Brodeur absorbed two incredible heart punches in his first real year in the NHL and went on to be, some would argue, the greatest goalie of All-Time; clearly one of the top-five winningest of All-Time. And that was amazing to me, covering those teams.

"They just kept going. It wasn't just guys like Daneyko and Stevens, who were just hard as nails, guys who would keep going. It was emotional guys like Richer. Bernie Nicholls, who couldn't play in the middle games in that series because he had a bad knee, then came back and played in Game 7. And they dominated Game 7. They outshot the Sabres something like 46 to 28 or something," (they actually outshot Buffalo 46-18 in Game 7), "and they only 2-1 because Hasek was crazy. But those were the Devils.

"Those were the things about that game that made it amazing to me. It was, 'how do you absorb that punch and comeback two nights later and win. And win as convincing a 2-1 game as you can possibly win."

MOST UNFORGETTABLE DEVILS MOMENT

JOHN DELLAPINA: "I don't think a Devils fan will like this, but they have to put it in perspective of my tenure on the Devils' beat, which ended after the '94 playoffs. So, while I covered the '95 series and their subsequent wins in 2000 and 2003, I wasn't their beat writer. When I was their beat writer, it was playoff endings. And they weren't wins. So it was that room in the 'Aud' with water on the floor, my feet being wet and exhaustion around me. And (also) the devastation in The Garden after Game 7. Those are my snapshots of covering the Devils."

38

5 ROLAND DRATCH (MSG NETWORKS)
MARTIN BRODEUR IS THE ALL-TIME WINNINGEST GOALIE IN
NHL HISTORY (@PRUDENTIAL CENTER)
MARCH 17, 2009
NJD 3, CHI 2

BACKGROUND

On any given night throughout the NHL season you can flip through the channels on your television and tune into a New Jersey Devils telecast. After all, the Devils do play 82 games during the regular season, with six others in the pre-season and, more often than not, at least one round of playoff games.

But one thing that many Devils fans don't realize is the amount of work that goes into those telecasts. It's not as simple as pointing a camera at the ice and letting the announcers tell you what's going on.

Rather, it's a whole production, with dozens of people involved on a nightly basis. There's even a 53-foot long, state-of-the-art truck that acts as the central hub for all the information and transmissions that go on during the pre-game, the game and the post-game.

And then there's the production crew. There are Graphics Coordinators, Directors, Stats people, Camera people, the Broadcasters; the list goes on and on. Oh, and last but certainly not least, the Producer.

I'm not going to attempt to list every single person who plays a role in the Devils' telecasts -- I'd be going on all night. But special mentions must be made for the following: Tom Meberg, Larry Gaines, Dennis Frasier, Erika Wachter, Steve Cangialosi, Ken Daneyko, Bryce Salvador and their esteemed Producer, Roland Dratch, all of whom pour their heart and soul into the production aspect of Devils games.

However, while there has been some turnover throughout the years, there has been one CONSTANT and that is Roland Dratch.

Dratch has been around the Devils since they landed in New Jersey in 1982, first as a fan and then later -- and to this day -- as a Producer.

But how did he get here? And why has he stayed for so long?

ROLAND DRATCH: "I grew up in Fort Lee, New Jersey, right over the George Washington Bridge. A lot of my buddies got into stock brokering and accounting and some guys wanted to be doctors and I just said to myself, 'you know, I just love TV and I love sports.' I said, 'let me give it a whirl.'

"I think, when I was in high school, everybody was looking at different fields and stuff. I said to myself, 'all kidding aside, I watch a lot of TV and most of its sports.' And I always went to Baseball games with my Father and Football games and watching Hockey on TV. I became a Devils fan in 1982, when they got there. I was a sophomore in high school and that's when I really fell in love with Hockey, when I went to see it live and I just kept saying to myself 'that's where I would want to be.'

"I started by going to school at Adelphi University in Garden City from 1984-1988. And I just realized, I was looking at all the different Majors and I said to myself, 'I wanted to have a job in television.' And then, about my senior year, at the time, a company called SportsChannel New York, that would become FOX New York and then eventually become MSG. I got a job there and they trained me to produce for four years. And then, eventually I got the job to be the Devils' Producer in 1995. And I've had it ever since.

"I've always loved live TV. A lot of people, some people like editing, some people like different things, being behind the camera. I wanted to be in the truck and I just loved everything about it. The excitement, the adrenaline rushes. And once I got into the truck, it might've been in 1990, I knew right away what I wanted to do.

"And it worked out. It's a tough thing. I would say that to anybody. The hours, I think people don't realize, to do a show at seven o'clock at night, you're there at 10:00 AM and you're walking into your car around 11-11:30 PM. So it's a lot of dedication. Then there's the travel and for six months it's pretty crazy. But I wouldn't change anything.

"Of course, it didn't necessarily have to be Hockey. When they trained me, I should have mentioned this, they trained me on the New York Mets because SportsChannel had the Mets, the Islanders, the Nets and the Devils. And they also had the Yankees for a while. So I just lucked out that the first opening that opened up was the Devils."

40

As a side note, while Roland professed himself to be a Devils fan, he also mentioned how he loved Football. So when I asked him whether he rooted for the Jets or the Giants he gave me a rather surprising answer -- as only he could.

ROLAND DRATCH: "I'm a huge Miami Dolphins fan. I'm a huge NFL fan. I've been to nine Super Bowls. I just love watching Football.

"I have a lot of relatives down in Florida. So when I was six-years-old, my Uncle and my Father took me to the Orange Bowl and we saw a Jets-Dolphins game. They all said, 'okay, so now you're going to root for the Jets.' And I said, 'no, I'm rooting for that team (the Dolphins).' Granted, this was me watching Don Shula, Bob Griese and Larry Csonka."

Thankfully he got a career in Hockey, because something tells me his backstory wouldn't fly with Jets and Giants fans. But let's get back on track.

MOST UNFORGETTABLE DEVILS GAME

You instantly knew he was going to be something special.

That is the sentiment that has been conveyed by just about anybody who watched Martin Brodeur as a rookie during the 1993-94 season. Whether it was scouts, broadcasters, writers, coaches, opponents or fellow teammates, the ever-humble Brodeur always seemed to marvel those who watched him perform.

And at 21-years-old, you just knew he was destined for big things. Of course, there were some speed bumps along the way, like the Devils' quadruple overtime loss to Buffalo in game 6 of the opening round of the 1993-94 playoffs. Or the heartwrenching series that was the Devils Eastern Conference matchup against the Rangers, also during the 1993-94 playoffs.

But that was one thing about Brodeur, he always bounced back. Heck, not even a work stoppage in the fall of '94, that lasted into the early Winter of '95 could deter this marvelous goaltender.

Once the lockout was lifted and the NHL returned to normalcy, Brodeur, in his first year as the undisputed No. 1 goalie for the Devils, quickly led his team to an impressive Stanley Cup championship over the powerhouse Detroit Red Wings.

And once he had a taste of success, he wanted more. And he got more, as Brodeur backstopped New Jersey to two more Stanley Cup championships in 2000 and 2003.

Of course, by the time the champagne had been drunk following the Devils' third Cup win in nine-years, Brodeur was more than halfway to the All-Time record for career wins by a netminder.

Martin Brodeur grew up idolizing Montreal Canadiens' goalie, Patrick Roy. And when Roy hung up his skates, with 551 career regular season wins to his name, he was the NHL's All-Time winningest goaltender. But it was a distinction he wouldn't hold for very long, as Brodeur was rapidly ascending the wins list.

Following the 2002-03 season -- Brodeur's 10th in the league -- Marty had amassed 365 wins, just 186 shy of Roy's record. And at the age of 30, Brodeur still had plenty left in the tank.

The chase was on and not even a lockout that cancelled the ENTIRE 2004-05 season could derail Brodeur's momentum. As long as he stayed healthy, there was no reason Brodeur wouldn't eventually catch Roy.

For several years, Hockey analysts attempted to predict when Brodeur would finally assume the mantle of the NHL's All-Time winningest netminder. They didn't have to wait long.

When the Devils and Brodeur opened the 2008-09 season, Marty was just THIRTEEN wins from tying the record -- 14 from calling the record his own.

In a normal year that would have meant Brodeur would likely have made history somewhere around the middle of November.

But this was not a normal year as Marty was plagued by an elbow injury that cost him more than three full months. After suffering the injury on November 1, 2008, against Atlanta, Brodeur did not return to the Devils until February 26, 2009, now just seven wins from tying Roy atop the leaderboard. And that meant that everybody was on high alert for the eventual historic achievement.

And with most Devils games being broadcast on MSG Networks, that meant Roland Dratch and his crew had to be prepared at all times.

ROLAND DRATCH: "Seeing Marty break the record was going to be special. Doing the Devils for all these years, we never did Stanley Cup games because it would always become a network game. But we would do a couple of rounds and the one thing that was always interesting is like, playoff Hockey is amazing, as you well know.

"But to watch him, having seen his whole career and to finally see him (get the record), you felt like you were part of history. Him tying Roy in Montreal and then coming back and beating the Blackhawks at home on Saint Patty's Day and the way we covered it, that's something I'll never forget. It's always something that's really special.

"We prepared for about a month before. Now, you can't pick the opponent. But you have to say, 'if this happens on the road, this is what we're going to do. If this happens at home, this is what we're going to do.' How many cameras? Are we going out onto the ice? Can we get Marty right away? Was his family in the crowd? It's like a checklist of just preparing. You can never know what happens. We didn't know he was going to cut the net.

"We didn't know he was going to skate around and do a victory lap. But you have to be prepared. And that's a key thing about any of this, even if it's not a big event, is your preparation. A lot of people don't know. They don't know how many cameras we have or how many tape machines, or the volume. It's a 26-person crew every night. But on that night, we were prepared, I would say for roughly about five weeks."

All that preparation paid off as Brodeur inched closer to Roy. And when the Devils arrived in Montreal, with history in the offing, it all felt like it was going to pay off.

ROLAND DRATCH: "I think we all felt honored and we all felt happy that we were going to be a part of it. But you also don't want to screw it up. You don't want to miss anything. I think people really feel proud of what they do in their careers. That whole crew worked so many years together and rooting for the team too. You want to see something happen and you want to be the ones doing it. It's a sense of pride and you don't care about how long you're there for, how long the telecast is. But you want to just make sure that it's done correctly. And I think the whole crew, as much as Marty was celebrating, we were celebrating in the truck. Again, you're part of it. You can always go back and tell people, 'I remember I worked that night.'"

With Patrick Roy in attendance, Brodeur bested his childhood team -- in front of his idol -- by securing a 3-1 victory, making 22 of 23 saves in the process.

That was March 14, 2009. The Devils' next game wasn't until March 17, when they would host the Blackhawks in front of what was expected to be a sold out crowd.

Equaling Patrick Roy was one thing (and a fantastic achievement at that), but to call the record his own, Brodeur was going to have to secure ONE. MORE. WIN. Would the Devils' netminder be up to the tasking, knowing full well that if he didn't do it against Chicago he was going on a long road trip that would likely see him break the record in what would probably be hostile territory?

ROLAND DRATCH: "I got a lot of sponsors that day. You're still doing a telecast after all. At that time too, Patrik Elias was going to have a milestone. (Elias was on the verge of becoming the franchise's

All-Time points leader). So you want to make sure you don't shortchange Patrik."

And that milestone occurred late in the second period as Elias setup Brian Gionta for the Devils third goal of the game. The assist by Elias on Gionta's short-handed goal may have seemed like icing on the cake in the moment. But it would prove to be extremely valuable in short order, as Chicago stormed back with a power-play just 32 seconds later, courtesy of Cam Barker.

Barker's tally brought the Blackhawks within 3-1 as the teams headed into the third period.

ROLAND DRATCH: "I think for the first two periods you're pumping it up, you're getting everyone ready for the possibility (of Marty breaking the record).

"But when that third period began, I made sure it was just all about the record. I got rid of the trivia question and the answer. I got rid of a lot of sponsorships. I got rid of all that stuff. As the Producer, now I said, 'when that third period begins, remember what we're doing here. We ride the wave to the end.' And again, it's teamwork. It's a game plan."

With Roland and his crew primed for a celebration, the Devils did their best to make sure that Brodeur's night would end with a win. But it wasn't easy as each team was assessed three penalties throughout the final period. And when Chicago's Dustin Byfuglien scored with just 2:03 remaining, it looked like the "game plan" might have to go out the window.

ROLAND DRATCH: "You don't want to lose track of it. We had two cameras on Marty, so now you're not going to lose Marty. When it (the clock) hits zero, he's going to go crazy. You've got a camera that's ready to get the Devils' reactions as they're going to pour over and go to Marty. But, you also keep saying to everyone, 'remember what the score is.' That's a big line in a TV truck. Remember the event. If it's 6-2, you could be more relaxed. Well, since it was a one-goal, it was a tight game. You don't want to be caught with egg on your face."

I'm sure the Blackhawks would have liked to put egg on the faces of the Devils and their fans. But Brodeur was having none of it. And with the final seconds draining off the clock, he made ONE. FINAL. SAVE on a shot from Troy Brouwer to secure the record and set off a well-deserved celebration.

ROLAND DRATCH: "It's a funny thing. I don't think we got into it until maybe a half-hour after the game was over, because it's just such a thing that when the clock hit zero, we were just so focused on what we were doing next. We had to get those cameras out on the ice and had to make sure that we were getting everything, making sure we're not losing anything. Were we going to get Marty for an interview? So it's rough until you catch your breath during that first break. Then you finally realize, 'wow, this is awesome! He broke the record!'

"You could see him smiling constantly. You saw how thrilled he was, the emotion. And the thing that I love personally, as the Producer, if you look at the video, all the lights are on. So we kept shooting the crowd, all these Devils fans with Number 30 on their jerseys. Them celebrating. People crying. The signs they're holding. It was so special that it ended in New Jersey, so all the Devils fans got that. And that was part of the whole theme too, that here you are, he did it at the Meadowlands, at the Rock, in front of the fans."

A PICTURE IS WORTH 1,000 WORDS

ROLAND DRATCH: "It would be the inside of the truck, with all the monitors. Just the whole crew, us facing forward and a monitor wall with 50 monitors. We spend a lot of time in the truck. I mean, I probably have done over 2,000 games. That's our home away from home. That's television."

ALL-STAR DEVILS PRODUCTION TEAM

It's an old Sailor's saying that a Captain is nothing without his crew. And while the Devils' production crew has not, at least to my knowledge, attempted to sail a boat, their Producer is very much like their Captain. And so, here are Roland's All-Time Production All-Stars.

ROLAND DRATCH: "Larry Gaines would have to be first. Larry's been with me since 1995. Larry runs the tape room and he's probably the hardest working man in television. My career would be nothing without him. He's just exceptional. He never stops. I've had the greatest privilege and honor to have the two best directors. That's all I've had next to me. Joe O'Rourke and now Tom Meberg. They've been great. I guess next I would have to go next to the announcers. It's a family. Matt Loughlin is a family member. And Cangy too. But the greatest thing was that I always rooted for Ken Daneyko and now I can call Dano my friend.

"I've been working with Dano since 2003 and he has been amazing. And I love Chico Resch. When Chico came here and then to be close with Chico, he's like an Uncle. He's just a great guy, like a family member who comes over for Thanksgiving or the Jewish holidays and you look forward for him to walk through the door. So I think I've just been very fortunate about my crew, that it's not only people to work with, but it's a true family. You spend so many hours together that it's like an old line, we probably spend more hours together than we do with our own families."

FUNNIEST DEVILS MOMENTS

What's the fun of working in television if you can't enjoy the occasional lighthearted moment? After all, you spend so much time with your crew that sometimes you need to break things up with a good laugh or two.

Of course, you might want to keep the laughter offset as it can occasionally bleed into Live TV, which, depending on how you look at things is either really good or really bad.

So here's Roland's choice for the funniest moments he's ever witnessed as the Producer of Devils games.

ROLAND DRATCH: "It would have to be the story that Stan (Fischler) always tells. Him and Matty (Matt Loughlin), they were together in Philadelphia and during the pre-game show, there was a Priest who was the Philadelphia Flyers' Priest and Matty and Stan we're in a small studio. So, the Priest walked into our studio to hang his jacket and he walked right behind Stan and Matty, live on TV. They kept going and kept going. There's Matty and there's Stan and the Priest walks right behind them. We all started chuckling in the truck. I guess, afterwards, The Father knew what he did, so he just stood offset.

"Then, about a half-hour later, when we were signing on the air, the background fell, right before we went on the air. So there's just a bare wall. And I hit the IFB, which is my communications to all the announcers and everyone in the truck. And I said, 'cue the Priest.' And Matty and Stan lost it. We came out of commercial break with Matty and Stan crying. Not laughing. Crying. They tried to talk and they started laughing harder. The amount of people that saw it -- it's a Devils-Flyers game -- and by the time they finally got composed, tears were running down their faces and when they threw it up to Doc (Emrick) and Chico, they were laughing to start the game. So I will always remember that one.

"I also remember once, Stan bit into an ice cream bar during a commercial break and his tooth went flying. So he moved his lip down to cover it. It was very, very funny."

6 MIKE " DOC" EMRICK (FOX)
*"THE CHAMPIONSHIP TO NEW JERSEY! THE DEVILS WIN THE STANLEY CUP!" (@*BRENDAN BYRNE ARENA)
JUNE 24, 1995
NJD 5, DET 2

BACKGROUND

First thing's first, congratulations to Mike "Doc" Emrick on his enshrinement into the Sports Broadcaster's Hall of Fame!

Most every Hockey fan has listened to "Doc" Emrick call a game at some point; after all, he is the Voice of the NHL's Playoff broadcasts.

But before Doc began plying his trade at the national level, he was the humble, energetic Voice of the New Jersey Devils television broadcasts. And for a man who grew up with very little exposure to Hockey and had a burning passion to become a Baseball announcer, that's a remarkable achievement.

DOC EMRICK: "Growing up in Indiana, I wanted to be a Baseball announcer because my exposure to Hockey was pretty limited. I grew up in rural Indiana in a town of 600. And our limitation was what we could see on television or hear on radio. And that was mostly Baseball and in the wintertime Basketball. But we had a team arrive about 45 miles away from us in Fort Wayne called the Komets, spelled with a 'K,' that is still there. And occasionally there would be games on television.

"CBS began broadcasting Saturday afternoon games in the late-'50s, prior to them broadcasting the 1960 Olympics. So I finally got to see some games on television and, of course, I knew we had a team in Fort Wayne that had been there for a while. So I started pestering my parents to take me to a game. And they did. The first time I saw hockey was December 10, 1960, and that was an epiphany moment for me, because I no longer wanted to be a baseball announcer. I wanted to broadcast Hockey."

Talk about having a change of heart! Of course, had Emrick not had his epiphany, the NHL and the Devils' broadcasts that have attracted fans for decades would have been very, very different.

DOC EMRICK: "So, then it was a question of how you get to do that (become a hockey announcer) when you're, 14-years-old and you're in rural Indiana. It was a process of going to games and sitting there with a recorder, like I'm sure a lot of people have told you they did. And going through college, I studied speech communication and minored in English at a place called Manchester College in Indiana, which is now Manchester University.

"Once I finished there, I had no experience in television. So I continued on in a Master's program at Miami University in Oxford, Ohio. And one thing that happened there, which I always tried to do was, it was one hour away from Dayton and having a credential for the campus station, I used that to attend every Dayton Gems IHL game that I could go to. I'd sit in the press box and get to know Hockey people a lot better and a record a few games to myself and send those tapes out.

"Of course, with no experience, no one hired me. But I was determined I was going to get into Hockey some way. So, now it's 1969, I sent all those tapes out and I got some nice rejection letters, which at that time you can appreciate, as there was no email. So those were actually mailed letters. I needed a job after I got my Master's degree and there was an opening for a Professor of Speech and Director of Broadcasting at a small college in western Pennsylvania called Geneva. It was 35 miles away from Pittsburgh.

"I got that job at $7,000 a year and because it was close to Pittsburgh, that kept my Hockey interest alive. I taught two days a week and managed the campus station there. And I went to the editor of the Daily Evening Newspaper and said, 'I'll cover the Penguins for free if you get me a pass.'"

Before anyone asks, 'why would he do it for free?' It wasn't -- and still isn't -- all that uncommon, as many well known Hockey writers and announcers started out this way.

DOC EMRICK: "So, the Editor said, 'sounds like a good deal to me.' So, that again got me inside the front door of dressing rooms and talking to people. So, after two years of teaching school, I realized that, 'hey, if this Hockey thing doesn't work out,' because I kept getting rejection letters with these tapes that I would send out, 'maybe I better go off and get an advanced degree so that I could earn $600 more per year with a Doctorate.

"I applied to two schools, Bowling Green in Michigan that had Doctoral programs in broadcasting and film, but also had campus stations that carried the University team's Hockey games. And as fate would have it, at Bowling Green, the guy who did the second periods, a student did the second periods, a staff member did the first and third, the guy who did the second periods -- the student -- graduated.

"So the staff member who did the first and third said, 'if you take the Assistantship at Bowling Green, without audition, you can do the second period.' Well, that made up my mind. So I went to Bowling Green and did 18 periods of Hockey, two-years in a row and took in all the course work and sent out all the tapes again. And this time it was a legitimate air check. And a station in Port Huron, Michigan, called and for $160 a week, I was a professional Hockey announcer in the IHL for the Port Huron Flags. And that was 46 years ago. And I've been at it ever since. So, that is, strangely to you, the short version of how I got to do this.

"I was four years in the IHL, three years in the American League and wound up going to the Flyers in 1980, because the farm team of the Flyers was in Portland, Maine, and I had put in three years there and the Flyers promoted me from within. I was in Philadelphia for three years and then the Devils hired me to do games at Madison Square Garden Network. So I was an employee of The Network. So that was how I got my first exposure with the Devils. They were not very good at that time. Chico Resch was their goaltender. Johnny MacLean was a rookie. Ken Daneyko was a rookie that was in 1983. They lost a lot of Hockey games during those years, but that was my first year with them."

MOST UNFORGETTABLE DEVILS GAME

When the Devils began life anew in the fall of 1982, they were a franchise that had not yet experienced the sort of success that would elevate it to the pantheon of great teams just over a decade later.

But as the years went on, New Jersey began to change its image and its culture. They went from perennial losers to perennial winners and it all started when Lou Lamoriello took over as General Manager in September of 1987.

First came the firing of Head Coach Doug Carpenter. Then came the hiring of new Bench Boss, Jim Schoenfeld. And then came the team's first ever playoff berth, which actually led to a Cinderella run that lasted all the way to the Eastern Conference Final.

From there the Garden Staters continued to evolve and improve. And in 1993, Lamoriello hired the man who would eventually be responsible for New Jersey's first championship, Jacques Lemaire.

Serving as Devils' Head Coach, Lemaire implemented the now famous "Trap System" that has been at the core of the Devils' identity for the better part of three decades. And under Lemaire, the Devils thrived.

They thrived so much in fact that they were able to rebound from a crushing double-overtime loss in Game 7 of the 1994 Eastern Conference Final against the Rangers to come back the following year and win it all.

Even though a lockout cost the NHL a large portion of its' regular season, the Devils didn't let that dampen their resolve. They qualified for the playoffs and made a run all the way to the Stanley Cup Final, in which, they would be matched up against the powerhouse Detroit Red Wings.

Did the Devils have any chance at beating the heavily favored Red Wings? Not if you listened to some Hockey analysts, one of whom boldly declared that New Jersey would forfeit Game 4 after losing the first three games of the series.

Well, maybe in some other parallel universe he ended up being correct. But not in this one.

It was the first time in franchise history that the Devils were playing for the coveted Stanley Cup. And who was there to broadcast the games to the Devils' fan base? You guessed it, Doc Emrick.

DOC EMRICK: "I was working for FOX then and we got to do Games 1 & 4, ESPN had Games 2 & 3. We did the first game in Detroit and if you recall, that entire year was a lockout year and the East did not play the West at all. So there was no tune up for those two teams against one another. It was just whatever scouting could take place would tell the teams what they could do against one another.

"The build up to The Final was that Detroit was this offensive juggernaut that was going to blow right through New Jersey and after the first three games, there would probably be a white flag of surrender and that would be it. Well, it didn't work out that way. And in the first game, I believe Stephane Richer scored and they had Detroit pretty well shutdown. Bill Clement, who was doing the series on ESPN, related to me later on, it was like Detroit after the first game said, 'okay, now we've seen them.' And after the second game said, 'boys were in trouble.'

"There were a couple of moments from those games that I certainly remember, one being Scott Niedermayer's goal in Detroit that pretty well cashed the Red Wings in, in Detroit and silenced the crowd.

"I was at the end of the rink, opposite from where he scored and I was standing there with Peter McNab, because we did post-shows and that was Game Two. It was not the game that I televised with John on FOX. We did Game 1 and then we watched Game 2 and then Game 3 in New Jersey. And then we did Game 4. But I was standing with Peter in the third period, when the game was still up for grabs and he said, 'the Devils are gonna win the Stanley Cup and it might be a sweep.' And Peter's very tall and I'm not. And I said, 'I beg your pardon?' I leaned in a little closer and he said, 'the Devils are gonna win this thing and it might be a sweep.' You know, I've always trusted players who have a sense of how teams match-up.

"Eddie Olczyk has also said things similar to me about other matchups. So I always pay attention when they say something because they sense when a matchup is just a mismatch. And he had that sense of it. Then, probably five minutes later on the clock, Scott Niedermayer scored that goal and the Devils were gonna win Game 2 and win two games in Detroit. And they were going home with the chance of executing the sweep that Peter had talked about.

"So, then the scene shifted to New Jersey and they (Detroit) got shut down again. But, I think going into the fourth game, it was a question of whether Detroit could muster something and take the series back to Detroit or whether the Devils would pull off not only one of the stranger upsets, but also be able to call it a sweep.

"The lead up to the game was the usual carefulness that the Devils approached everything with.

"And at the start, Detroit tried to play differently and actually got a lead. They were playing a little bit different style that wasn't as wide open. They were playing very carefully. They were almost replicating the Devils' style, it appeared to me defensively. And it was working. They actually got to lead in the game.

"But the Devils basically just had, not only the impetus of the crowd, but they also had this overwhelming ability to create turnovers and get goals."

The Devils used that impetus and ability to quickly turn the tide of the game as Shawn Chambers scored his first goal of the game -- the fourth of the opening period -- to tie the game at 2 heading into the first intermission.

From there the second period, and really the rest of the game, was all Devils. Neal Broten scored his second goal of the game at the 7:56 mark of the second period to give New Jersey a 3-2 lead. And it was a lead they would not relinquish. In fact, it was the final lead change of the 1994-95 NHL season.

So, the Devils headed into the third period with a 3-2 lead, looking for more. And they got more.

DOC EMRICK: "What I remember a lot was the play of Sergei Brylin, and also, Shawn Chambers, who had a couple of goals in the game. And in the third period, of course, this is the time that you start thinking about these things. In the third period, when Chambers scored to make it 5-2, it was okay to celebrate. John Davidson and I were doing the telecast and I did have written on my scorecard, Dick Enberg, the noted broadcaster always said, 'the best ad libs are written down, because sometimes you want to make sure that it comes out exactly that way. You don't want to leave it to whim.'

"And so, 'the championship to New Jersey, the Devils win the Stanley Cup,' was written on my scorecard in front of me, because the last thing you want to do is have a signature moment and all of a sudden it doesn't come out exactly the way that you had intended. So that part was written out and as it became apparent after the Chambers goal that the Devils we're going to win this thing and win it in a surprise sweep, John Davidson turned to me during one of our timeouts and he said, 'play this right Doc, you're going to remember it for a long-time,' because the previous year he had been doing the Rangers' telecasts. And that had been the last year that the local telecasters were allowed to work all the way through the Stanley Cup Final.

"It became the property of the National Rights Holders the year later, which coincidentally was the year John and I were working together on FOX. That was the first year that the agreement was made that the national broadcasters would have the rights to do the last two rounds. So by luck, the guy who wound up doing the Devils' games during the regular season was also the national broadcaster who got to do Game 1 & 4 and their last game, as it turned out, their clinching game in the playoffs.

"But he (John Davidson) turned to me and he said that. And then the one thing that probably was the most striking of all was our cameraman got a shot of Mike Peluso down at the bench and he was crying. He was so overwhelmed by the emotions of the moment, that he was openly crying and shedding tears of joy. And John noticed that he actually missed a shift with Bobby Holik and Randy McKay, the Crash Line.

"They became very famous as the Crash Line that year, because they were the unit that Jacques Lemaire would put out to sort of establish Devils' Hockey whenever it was needed. And John pointed that out. We showed him at the bench and even in the handshake line, you could still see he was sort of shaking his head back and forth, that massive, stringy long hair of his, shaking at the same time as he was trying to shake back the tears as he was shaking hands with members of the Red Wings. He was a genuinely good guy, Mike. And we always liked having chats with him because he was so much fun. But here was just a genuine moment where the whole shock of the situation was getting to him.

"And it was all part of it, the clearing of the puck and everything that got them down to the last minute and the announcement by Bob Arsena at one minute to go. Everything brought a thunderous cheer. And then they rushed off the bench and they dislodged the net behind Marty Brodeur, pushed that into the backboards as they celebrated.

"That was all part of a great memory. But that's the thing that struck me the most out of all those games that I got to broadcast during those years. I've always pointed to the seventh game of the Conference Final in Philadelphia in 2000, although I was not broadcasting that one. That was one of the more overwhelming victories because it came from 3-1 down.

"But this was one that I did get to broadcast and it was just, because it turned out to be the fourth game of The Final. I wouldn't have done the fifth game. But I did get to do the fourth and the Devils won it and it was their first of three championships during a time that I was just lucky to be there.

"So, that's one of the things that you really never forget. And then, because of Devils' dressing room was so small, by the time Peter and I had done our post-game after Game 4 for SportsChannel, we walked down through the stands and the Devils' room was jammed. There were people still out in the hallway hoping to get in.

"I just stood down at the end of the hallway, probably 40 feet down the hallway, outside the room and was just chatting with some people. And this was probably an hour, an hour-and-a-half after the game. And Scott Stevens came down the hallway with the Stanley Cup. Everybody was dressed up, they were going somewhere for a post Stanley Cup party. And one thing you never forget, he walked down the hallway with the Stanley Cup and he walked over to me with it and let me touch it.

"I wasn't going to pick it up or do anything like that, but he just let me see it, close up and touch it. And then he walked on and that was very nice of him."

MOST UNFORGETTABLE DEVILS MOMENT

DOC EMRICK: "It would be hard to pair it down to just one moment. I guess it would probably be the banner raising of the first championship, the following Fall. It would be very hard to take it down to one, because there are so many glorious moments. You'd have Marty Brodeur cutting up the net from being the winningest goaltender of All-Time. You'd have Scott Stevens' jersey retirement, because that was the first one and the Devils acknowledging individual achievements. And Scott was the very first one.

"It would be hard to do one, but I think that would be what I would pick, for the same reason that out of all of the telecasts, I picked the fourth game of the '95 championship, when they finally won a championship for the first time, because that was finally getting to the mountain top. And then the rest was establishing the excellence that they built toward. We got a hint of it the previous year when they took the Rangers to a seventh game and ended in double-overtime."

7 STAN FISCHLER (SPORTSCHANNEL)
YELLOW SUNDAY: "HAVE ANOTHER DONUT" (@BRENDAN BYRNE ARENA)
MAY 8, 1988
NJD 3, BOS 1

BACKGROUND

"The Hockey Maven," Stan Fischler, is known across the NHL as one of the brightest minds in the game. His nearly seven decades worth of experience, accumulated as both a writer and as a television analyst, are second to none; especially when it comes to the New York/New Jersey area.

Stan Fischler has authored over a 100 books, most of them hockey related, and has earned numerous accolades during his time covering the New York Rangers, New York Islanders and of course, the New Jersey Devils. Oh, and let's not forget about his stint broadcasting games for the Hartford Whalers.

While "The Maven," hung up his microphone following the 2017-18 season, he still keeps himself active as a prominent hockey historian for the NHL's website, as well as for the Islanders' website; consistently creating various forms of material for fans to learn about the great game of hockey.

But before he became "The Hockey Maven," -- a nickname given to him by current Vancouver Canucks Head Coach, Travis Green, when Green was still an active player -- he was just another kid from Brooklyn, New York, who was fascinated by the game of hockey.

"I went to my first game at The Garden in 1939, when I was seven," said Fischler. "And I instantly became enthralled with the game. But I was too young to go to the Rangers' games, so I went to the Rovers' games -- they had double headers on Sunday afternoons. The

Rovers were really terrific. There were MET League games, which were local players. It was not limited by age and there were four teams: the Sands Point Tigers, Manhattan Arrows, The Jamaica Hawks and The Stock Exchange Brokers, who became The Brooklyn Torpedoes during World War II.

"There was a wonderful preliminary game at 1:30 and then at 3:30 the Rovers would play. The Rovers were the Rangers' farm team in the Eastern League. Just excellent hockey, exciting, I loved it. Rangers games at that time started at 8:30, so my parents wouldn't let me go because it was too late and I had school the next day. So I didn't go to a Rangers game until 1942.

"In '42, for my 10th birthday, my parents gave me a little Philco Radio, it was called the Transitone and a scrapbook with an Indian Head -- it had a three dimension Indian Head on it. Those were the catalysts for my love of hockey. With the radio, I was able to pick up Canadian games from Toronto, with Foster Hewitt announcing. He was very, very exciting, so I became a Leafs fan just by listening to him. To this day, there has not been an announcer to equal Foster Hewitt the way he called a game. There are a lot of wonderful announcers, but Foster was The Dean.

"With the scrapbook, I started to clip stories out of the papers, which, at that time, were just the New York papers. So in 1942, the clippings started. And this was all part of my hockey infatuation. I was an only child, so hockey was like my brother in a way. It gave me something to do. I still have every scrapbook, starting with 1942. It was a different type of hockey journalism. It wasn't as intense as it is now, but it was more fun.

"By the 1946-47 season, when I started High School, I was a crazy Leafs fan. Once, I was down at Times Square going to see a movie at The Paramount with my friend Howie Sparer and while I was waiting for him I was standing at 43rd between Broadway and 7th, where the old Times building was. At the bottom there was an out of town newspaper stand. It was a big deal; there were papers from all over the country and Canada.

"While I was waiting for Howie, I saw there was a newspaper called *The Toronto Globe and Mail*, it was only a quarter. I picked up the paper, turned to the sports section and saw all these hockey stories that weren't in the New York papers. Of course, the main stories were about The Leafs. I was amazed. It was like I was discovering gold.

"That night, I went home and opened up to the Editorial page and saw I could subscribe and it wasn't that much. So I subscribed and everyday, one day after it came out, I was getting it in my mailbox; I was only getting *The Globe* one day late. The stories and the writing were wonderful. I found one particular columnist named, Jim Coleman, who I emulated in my head, because I loved his style. I had all his columns in my scrapbooks. I had one scrapbook for every year and it was all Leafs. That was the year they won their first Cup out of three in a row (1946-47).

"By now, I was old enough to go to the Rangers games, which I did. My friend Jimmy and I became season ticket holders -- End Balcony section 333, row E, seats five and six. Just wonderful seats at The Old Garden, the End Balcony. Before that, when I was going to the Rovers' games, I would get a program and it had a lot of white space and on the roster page there was also a lot of white space. So, at the end of every game, I'd write stories on my own, which, in retrospective, was an indication that I liked to write.

"When my teams won it was a wonderful story. But when my teams lost, it was the referee's fault. I couldn't write hockey in High School, I did very little writing in High School. When I got to Brooklyn College in 1950, we didn't have a (hockey) team, but we did have a soccer team and I got to write about them. Soccer was very big and it was a great experience. That, plus one journalism course, taught by Phil Leddy -- no relation to Nick Leddy on the Islanders -- who was the professor had a profound influence on me.

"So, in 1951, the Leafs won their fourth Cup in five years. Bill Barilko scored the winning goal, he had been my hero. But then he disappeared in a plane crash -- him and another guy. They were heading to the fishing area in Northern Ontario when they disappeared. They didn't find them for 10 years.

"I remained a Leafs fan through the 1951-52 season, but by that time, Herb Goren had become the Rangers' press agent and he formed a Rangers' Fan Club. I went to the first meeting; they had a few players there. It was very exciting. And I said, 'wow, this is for me.' So, myself, along with two other guys -- Fred Meier, who I'm still in touch with (we played roller hockey together) and Jerry Weiss -- decided to put together a Fan Club paper -- The Rangers' Review.

"At that time, the PR guy, Herb Goren, who formed the Fan Club -- it wasn't fans who did it, it was the Rangers -- allowed us access to the players. The first guy we wanted to interview was Eddie Kullman and he was a good, tough, checking forward. A lot of the players, the day of the game, stayed at the old Belvedere Hotel, which was across the street from The Old Garden. So, Freddy and me went up, before Kullman took his pre-game nap and we interviewed him. He was wonderful. We couldn't believe it.

"Then, as the Fan Club grew, I stopped being a Leafs fan and I became a Rangers fan and I became the Vice President of the Fan Club. Gradually, with all the writing, I had access to all the players and The Garden; I was also going to all the Rovers' games. And I knew the guy who ran the Rovers. His name was Tommy Lockhart, who was also a business manager for the Rangers. So, one day, I went to Tommy and I suggested that I write a newsletter about the whole Eastern League. It was very important to me and it would cost them nothing. So he said do it and every week he'd distribute my stuff.

"So, when I graduated from Brooklyn College in 1954, that September, Herbie Goren offered me a job in publicity, as his assistant. It was like the old cliché, like dying and going to heaven."

And after getting a foothold in New York, Fischler quickly became a household name with his various columns on all things NHL. Eventually, Fischler transitioned to television -- while still keeping up his writing -- and was working Islanders games.

But when the Devils came knocking he couldn't resist, taking on the double duty of broadcasting Devils and Islanders games.

STAN FISCHLER: "Well, my original company doing the Islanders games was SportsChannel. And SportsChannel eventually got the contract -- beating out MSG -- for the Devils; they put me on both (Devils and Islanders). On the Devils' side I worked with Al Albert, Marv's younger brother. He did the play-by-play and I did the color. And this was the year before Lou Lamoriello came in as G.M. (1986-87).

"The year of the big snow game, that's when we started. We may have done two games for two years together, but that's how I started with the Devils. And I was doing the Devils in 1987-88 when they made the playoffs for the first time."

MOST UNFORGETTABLE DEVILS GAME

The 1987-88 season was one of great change for the New Jersey Devils. They had a new General Manager in Lou Lamoriello, who also hired a new Head Coach towards the end of the regular season by the name of Jim Schoenfeld. And, last but not least, the Devils qualified for the playoffs for the first time in their history -- on the last day of the season no less.

So there were the Devils, a surprising, yet intriguing entrant in Lord Stanley's Playoffs.

First they knocked off the Islanders in a hard fought six-game series. Then they outlasted the Capitals in seven. So, not only were these Devils a surprise for making it into the playoffs, they were now shocking the entire NHL by reaching the Eastern Conference Final; where they would face the Boston Bruins.

If New Jersey could beat the Islanders AND the Capitals, surely they must be considered a threat to do the same thing against the Bruins, right? And through the first three games of the series they alternated wins and losses, with Boston ahead two games to one in the best-of-seven series.

But there was an incident after Game 3 that threw the series into chaos.

Shortly after the Devils completed their 6-1 loss, Head Coach Jim Schoenfeld attempted to confront Referee Don Koharski about several calls he felt went against his team. And after waiting in the runaway near New Jersey's locker room, Schoenfeld finally got his chance to speak his mind.

While yelling at Koharski, Schoenfeld said, "You're crazy, you're crazy. You fat pig. Go have another doughnut."

Had their exchange ended right then and there, perhaps fences would have been mended and no further issues would have arisen. But no, this was just getting started. Depending on who you talk to and who you believe, Schoenfeld either shoved Koharski down to the ground or Koharski simply tripped over his own two feet. Either way, things had been taken up a notch.

STAN FISCHLER: "Yellow Sunday was inevitable. There's never been anything like it in so many different ways. And the fact of the matter was that Yellow Sunday came about because of the previous game, where Referee Koharski, I believe that it was one of the worst officiated games I'd ever seen against the Devils. And, of course, Jim Schoenfeld being the coach was furious.

"Now, a referee using common sense and who had been around would have understood that Schoenfeld was furious. It's a bad loss. It's playoffs. And at the end of the game, Schoenfeld was at the boards yelling at Koharski. Now, what Koharski should have done was retreated or stayed at center ice. Eventually, what happened was that, instead of staying where he was, or just avoiding any contact or any confrontation, he comes along and he goes right up to Schoenfeld and they're going back and forth.

"Well, what Schoenfeld did was the natural reaction. What the referee should have done was not light a match with the dynamite. He should have stayed where he was. So now, and you have to understand, our studio was right next to where all of this was happening.

"And then, they both started down the corridor and, of course, the big lie was that, or at least I thought it was, was that Shoenfeld pushed him, which he did not do. What happened was that Koharski missed the step and he fell. Then they resumed with 'have another donut you fat pig.' And this was right by where we were. So I was there and as I said, I felt Schoenfeld got a bum deal because of that.

"But the episode then boiled over because Shoenfeld wasn't suspended. And the other part of it was that the President John Ziegler, nobody knew where Ziegler was. This led up to the game on Sunday and it was a sell out. It was Mother's Day. My wife Shirley was there and there was a great deal of tension; starting in the morning.

"Then the word came down that the referee and the two linesmen refused to work the game. And now there was a question about, 'well, what's the league going to do, because Ziegler was nowhere to be found.' Nobody knew where Ziegler was. The second in command was Brian O'Neill and I believe Brian was in Montreal, that's where the League Headquarters were then. Brian O'Neill may have been a factor here, but the whole point was whether the game would be played now or not.

"It was finally decided that if you're going to have a game and the officials are on strike, well then somebody's got to do something. You've got to get officials; you need to get a ref and two linesmen. And as it happened, there were three off-ice officials with a lot of experience.

"One was Jimmy Sullivan. One was Paul McInnis. And the other one was Vince Godleski. Anyhow, the three guys had been refereeing collegiate games, all kinds of stuff and they were very competent. They all played the game. Jimmy was the youngest. Vin and Paul McInnis were both off-ice guys from New Jersey and Jimmy was with the Islanders. So they were designated that, Jimmy would be one of the linesman. Vince was the other one. And Paul was the referee. Now the story gets complicated because here are these guys and nobody expected this to happen.

"They didn't have their own skates, which makes a huge difference. They had to borrow skates. They didn't have referee jerseys. So they put on these yellow practice ones. In the meantime, the place is packed. Nobody knows really what's going on.

"What happened was that Dr. McMullen, who owned the team, had political connections and the injunction regarding whether the game was going to be played or not was turned into the Devils' favor by this judge, who I think was in Jersey City. And that gave the green light for them to play the game. Meantime, it's way past what would've been the starting time and finally the game begins.

"And, of course, nobody knew how these guys would be as the officials. They didn't have their own skates. Nobody knew they were skating on somebody else's skates. So, we're doing the game and, of course, it's a partisan, a Devils crowd. Of course, the Bruins were fighting this whole thing. They didn't want to play. But now they're playing. And it turns out that there was a lot of nasty stuff."

Along with the "nasty stuff," the Devils jumped out to an early 2-0 lead as Dave Maley and Pat Verbeek scored 45 seconds apart midway through the first period.
And that only further incensed the Bruins.

STAN FISCHLER: "There were fights that had to be broken up and neither of the three guys were particularly big in terms of size; it wouldn't be easy for them to break up fights. Anyhow, the Devils went on and they won the game (3-1 was the final score) and from my viewpoint, the three replacement guys did a terrific job, under very, very tough conditions."

MOST UNFORGETTABLE DEVILS MOMENT

STAN FISCHLER: "Oddly enough, it was a negative one and it was in the same series. It was 1987-88, first time in the playoffs. (The Devils had) a lot of young guys: Kirk Muller and Pat Verbeek, a lot of good, fun guys. And we took them (the Bruins) to seven games. The seventh game was in Boston Garden and it was 0-0 in the first period. And the way the series unfolded, there was no question that the first goal in Game 7 was going to be huge.

"The line with, Kirk Muller, Verbeen and I think (Aaron) Broten -- I don't remember who the third one was -- anyway, that line came out like gangbusters and they were dominating. Finally, the puck came to Verbeek, in perfect position, in front of the net and Boston's goalie was Reggie Lemelin, who was a good goalie.

"It was a sure goal. I mean it was just, no doubt about it. I think what happened was that it may have gotten on his stick, in a rolling fashion. It wasn't flat. So it was like a split second that he had to tame it and take the shot. We expected it to be a goal and Lemelin made one of the greatest saves I've ever seen in my life. It's still in my head, you know, how did this happen? And, of course, he made the save and then the Bruins went on and scored.

"It was a very close game. In fact, Kenny Daneyko was a goat on one of the Bruin goals. But the Bruins got the first goal and they went on to win the game. And that, to me, was just heartbreaking. It was the difference between them winning and losing the series. They were so hot that. I mean, the club was in a position to go to The Final and that would've been a huge upset."

8 ANDREW GROSS (THE JOURNAL NEWS)
TALE OF THE TAPE: STEVE THOMAS VS. PHIL CROWE
(@BRENDAN BYRNE ARENA)
NOVEMBER 11, 1995
NJD 4, PHI 2

BACKGROUND

Paging Oscar Madison, I have a story for you.

For those of you who aren't familiar with the pop culture reference, Oscar Madison was a character in the hit 1970's sitcom, The Odd Couple and was portrayed by actor Jack Klugman. And Oscar's stated profession was that of a sports writer.

Now, you might be wondering to yourself, 'what does a character on a decades-old sitcom have to do with a book about the New Jersey Devils?'

Well, the answer is pretty straightforward, for you see, well-respected sports journalist, Andrew Gross drew inspiration from the Oscar Madison character when he was growing up. And Gross has done it all since following in the footsteps of the Odd Couple's resident sports writer.

In a career that has spanned parts of four decades, Gross has managed to cover various different sports and special events. And the most important sport he's covered has been hockey. As a one-time member of *The Journal News* and currently working for *Newsday*, Gross has covered ALL THREE Metropolitan area NHL teams -- the New York Islanders, the New York Rangers and, of course, the New Jersey Devils.

But how and why did Gross get to where he is today?

ANDREW GROSS: "It seems like it was the only thing I ever wanted to do with my life. When I was growing up, my dad was a reporter, editor, and eventually, the Editor-In-Chief of a trade publication, covering the textile industry. It was called *the Knitting Times*, but I just knew it as *The Times*. I liked to tell people my dad worked for *The Times* and I just remember being four, five, six-years-old and my dad would come home from work every day, say around 6-6:30 and he would bring the *New York Times* home with him.

"I just remember being a little kid, spreading *The Times* out on the floor, opening it up and literally crawling around and looking at the paper; looking at the standings and looking at the boxes. I just loved sports for as long as I can remember. And I just remembered also loving reading newspapers. When I went into sports media, people told me I had a really good voice for radio. Play-by-play announcers have told me that. But honestly, I never thought of doing anything except writing for a newspaper. It's really what I wanted to do. The overriding arc was I loved sports. I mean, if I could have been an athlete, that's what I would have done.

"But, luckily I was such a bad athlete that by 11 or 12, it was crystal clear to me that if I wanted to be in the ballpark when I grew up, I wasn't going to make it as an athlete. I wasn't going to be a baseball player or a hockey player. I had to figure out another way. Also, the other thing was there was a show called, The Odd Couple that was on, it was in syndication when I started watching it, but Oscar Madison was a sports writer on the show and he made that seem so glamorous. I grew up thinking, 'I'm going to be a sports writer. I'm going to have my own office. When I have a secretary, I'm going to go travel whenever and wherever I want; have a girlfriend in every town.'"

Again, paging Oscar Madison, I think you'll be pleased to know you did a heck of a job inspiring others to follow your lead.

ANDREW GROSS: "Obviously though, that's not what it's like. But I really romanticized the thought of being a sports writer. I was lucky enough that I can put two sentences together, which is, to me, an inherent skill. I think you either have it or you don't have it. I talked about my dad being a reporter and editor. My grandfather was also a Yiddish writer. He published seven books about living in the old country. My mom has done three books. So writing has pretty much been a constant through the family. So I kind of felt like I was going into the family business. I went to Syracuse University with the expressed intention of taking newspaper journalism. And I remember before my freshman year, before I had gone to a class at Syracuse, I had already gone to the student newspaper and signed up to be a writer there.

"I wound up working at the school newspaper all four years. I wound up being the Managing Editor and the Sports Editor; just had a great run there. I got a chance to cover the NCAA Final Four in New Orleans in 1987, Syracuse Vs. Indiana. I was covering Syracuse lacrosse. I worked really hard at Syracuse. But it was funny. I always wanted to be a baseball writer, not a hockey writer. In fact, when I got my first job out of Syracuse, I got a job in Oneonta.

"So I worked at *The Daily Star* there for four years and one of my college buddies got a job there too. One day we wrote a dual column and it was like, I wrote the 'why baseball is much better than hockey' and Rob wrote 'why hockey is much better than baseball.' And it's funny because I just caught up with Rob, he had moved to London and I hadn't seen him in about 15-20 years. We just caught up in Tampa last season. And one of the first things I said to him was, 'you know what? You were right.' Anyway, I'd always wanted to be a baseball writer and I did cover minor league baseball up in Oneonta, the Oneonta Yankees. And that allowed me to do some feature work at Yankee Stadium.

"I came down doing some features and I just remember in 1991, the Yankees were an awful team. Stump Merrill was the manager and I wound up at Yankee Stadium for a doubleheader against the Detroit Tigers, who were probably the only team worse than the Yankees at that time, on an August day when it was about 105 degrees. I just remember looking around the press box around the second inning of the second game and everyone was miserable. I mean all the sports writers were busy. They were complaining. No one was happy. There was one guy who was happy, but that's another story. And I just had an epiphany that I didn't want to be that person. I didn't want to be that miserable. I joke about baseball being better than hockey. But I did love hockey. I was a crazed hockey fan growing up in The City.

"I went to school 10 blocks from Madison Square Garden and I got beat up everyday because I would come into school with my Billy Smith jersey on. But hockey always held a really special place (in my heart). So, to fast forward, I'm working at *The Journal News* in Rockland, in Westchester and I was doing a lot of backup baseball. I did some Devils games. We didn't really cover the Devils, but for home games they would send a reporter down. So I talked my way into doing a couple of those games. Then, in 1999, they gave me the St. John's Basketball beat, which was a travel beat. And I did almost four years of that.

"Then, in 2003, Rick Carpiniello, who was on the Rangers' beat, he was promoted to being a columnist and they came to me and they said, 'we would like you to become the Rangers beat writer.' And honestly, I told them, 'I'm going to need a little time to think about it.' At the time, my older daughter was only six and my younger daughter was still two. And I said, 'I don't know if I can do this to my family, being on the road as much as this would entail.' So I came back the next day to my editor and I said, 'I don't know about this.' And he goes, 'I understand your concerns here. Let me put it in another way. I can always guarantee that there's going to be a Rangers beat at this paper. I can't guarantee there's going to be a St. John's beat.' I said, 'oh, okay. Well, let me introduce myself as the new Rangers writer.'"

As "The Maven," Stan Fischler always likes to say, "health and family first." However, sometimes work has to be thrown into the mix, otherwise, you might have some difficulty providing for your family.

ANDREW GROSS: "So, I wound up going to The Record, in New Jersey in 2007. And in 2008 they put me back on the Rangers beat. And Tom Gulitti, was our Devils beat writer and he was fantastic. For a long time the two of us were a really good team. He would do Devils and I would do Rangers. He was probably the hardest worker I've ever seen and I would just try and keep up with the amount of copy he put out. Then, he got a job with *NHL.com* down in Washington and I covered the Rangers through the 2015 Eastern Conference Final against Tampa.

"The Devils was their big beat and they said, 'look, Tom has established so much with the Fire and Ice Blog, his reporting was unbelievable.' And they came to me and said, 'look, we really don't want to open this up. We really only see one person being able to step into Tom's shoes.' I was like, 'that's great. Who?' And they were like, 'you're on the Devils.' For that off-season, I was actually covering the Devils and the Rangers.

"The honest story of how I became the official Devils writer is that Gannett bought *The Bergen Record* and Gannett also owned *The Journal News*. So, Gannett was going to consolidate everything. And at the time, I was still technically the Rangers beat writer for The Bergen Record and Rick Carpiniello was still technically the Rangers beat writer for *the Journal News*. So, they had a big meeting with all the editors at these papers to consolidate everything. And they went on a board and they were like, 'okay, the Rangers, who do we got?' And one editor said, 'we have Rick Carpiniello, he's been doing it since like 1979.' Then my editor at *The Record* said, 'okay, we have Andrew Gross, he's been doing it since 2008.'

"So then, Gannett looked and said, 'okay, Carpiniello is on the Rangers beat and we can lay off Andrew.' And my editor stepped up and said, 'no, no, no, no. What I meant to say is Andrew is on the Devils beat.' And they said, 'okay, Andrew can keep his job.' So that's how I got the Devils beat at *The Record*.

"That was John Hynes' second season. He had had an okay first season and then his second season, my first season on the beat, which was Taylor Hall's first year with the team, was just an unmitigated disaster. I think they won three games combined in February, March and April. It was a train wreck of a season, but that was my first season on the beat. That's how I came to be the Devils beat writer. And I actually didn't even make it through two seasons. I did one full-season when they were bad. And then the second season, Taylor Hall's MVP season, I left the Devils beat like March 1st of that year."

And after leaving the Devils beat, Gross moved on to the Islanders beat with *Newsday*, where he has been providing superb coverage ever since.

MOST UNFORGETTABLE DEVILS GAME

The 1995-96 incarnation of the Devils saw the team suffer from a Stanley Cup hangover. After winning it all against Detroit in the spring of '95, New Jersey entered the new season in the Fall of '95 looking to become a repeat Cup champion. But things didn't go as they had planned, for the Garden Staters missed out on the playoffs for the first time since the 1988-89 campaign. And it would be the last time they missed out on the post-season until the 2010-11 season.

But let's not get ahead of ourselves.

When the 1995-96 campaign began the Devils had a target on their backs. As the defending champs, every team was out to get them and to prove themselves worthy as challengers to the throne.

And after a 7-6-1 (7 wins, 6 losses, 1 tie) start, New Jersey hosted the Philadelphia Flyers on November 11, 1995, for a game that was sure to be as hard-hitting as possible. After all, this was the Flyers we're talking about, as Philadelphia was historically known for its bullying nature.

Now, normally an early season matchup like this wouldn't be much to write home about. The Devils won the game 4-2. There were a grand total of two fights (not uncommon back then). And Chris Terreri picked up the win in goal.

So why am I bringing up this game of all games?

Well, it was the first Devils game covered by a young sports writer known as Andrew Gross.

Gross was there on assignment and as green as could be. But it was his first step towards a long career-covering hockey.

ANDREW GROSS: "Honest to God, I didn't know anything about covering hockey, really didn't. And there were a lot of things that stuck out from that game. One thing, I didn't know that I was responsible for writing an early story for the early deadlines. So I got to the Meadowlands probably around 3:30-4 and I'm sitting there and one of the editors calls me and he goes, 'what do you got for an early?'

"And I was like, 'an early?' So I went to Mike Levine who was the PR guy and I said, 'I kind of need to talk to a player.' Now, this was back in the days where you had an hour, there was a media period from 4:30-5:30, where you could talk to a player. And I said, 'Mike, I know you don't know me, but I apparently screwed this up and I really don't want to lose my job on the first day. I need to talk to a player before the game.' And Mike was like, 'okayyy, who do you want?' And I looked out and I saw Esa Tikkanen doing his sticks, so I go, 'Esa Tikkanen would be fantastic to talk to.' And Mike looked at me and he rolled his eyes. He was like, 'hold on.' So he walked over and I could see him talking to Esa Tikkanen and I think Mike, to his credit, actually asked the question, 'will you talk to this kid?'

"The answer was, 'not a chance.' I mean, I knew nothing about Tikkanen and his personality. And now that he's retired, he's a great storyteller and he's a fun person to be around. But he was a lot off the ice, like he was on the ice, as a player and he was not going to talk to me. So they gave me Sergei Brylin. And I just remember that being a very (difficult interview). I don't know how much English he spoke at that time. So, I learned very early to have an early story and to go to the morning skate.

"Another thing I remember was that, in the Meadowlands, there were two press boxes. One was the greatest press box, maybe in NHL history. It was two sections in the middle of the stands, about 10 to 12 rows off the ice; right at center ice. It was unbelievable. I mean it was great. But I wasn't in that press box for the game. They had a second press box called the Halo. Yeah, it's exactly what it sounds like. You had to take an elevator up there. It was a catwalk basically on the metal and the ceiling. It was a long way up.

"And what I remember was, and again, I didn't know all these guys yet. I mean, now Colin Stephenson, who covers the Rangers for *Newsday* and did a lot of Devils work for *the Newark Star-Ledger* with Rich Chere. I mean he's been my friend now for going on two decades and now we're colleagues, we're teammates. I love this guy. But I didn't know Collin yet. But I read his hockey stuff in *the Daily News*. Now, Colin always gets embarrassed when I tell this story. But I looked at the seating chart and I saw I was sitting next to Colin Stephenson. And to me, I was like; I thought I'd made it to the big time.

"I was like, 'look at me, I'm sitting next to Colin Stephenson, this is fantastic.' So that's what I did. And I did cover more games at the Meadowlands, eventually making it down to the main press box. They started putting me down there when they started recognizing who I was.

"Meanwhile, the other thing I remember was, in that game, Steve Thomas, who was one of the nicest guys you could meet, was playing for the Devils and he got into a brawl with Phil Crowe. Crowe was this heavyweight and Steve was not a smaller guy, but he wasn't as big as the Flyers' behemoth. And the Flyers were known for their physical play. Stevie Thomas got the crap knocked out of him in the game."

Here's a quick tale of the tape.

The fight began at 7:16 of the first period and featured two players who were definitely in different weight classes. Steve Thomas (Devils) entered the bout measuring in at 5-10, 185lbs. And his opponent, Phil Crowe (Flyers) weighed in at 6-2, 230lbs. Not exactly a fair fight if you ask me.

ANDREW GROSS: "It came off a face-off where guys are pushing and shoving and the play went into the Flyers' zone. Then, behind the play, in the neutral zone, in front of the benches, all of a sudden you just saw Crowe get on top of Steve Thomas. And in most hockey fights, especially now with the visors, face shots aren't a thing. Mostly it's just grabbing. But Crowe got his left hand free and was machine-gunning Stevie Thomas in the face. It was bang, bang, bang, bang, bang. And Thomas actually went down almost to his knees and then he got up and the refs still didn't step in. That's when Stevie was able to throw in a couple of shots of his own.

"So, at the end, it wasn't as one-sided a fight as it started out as, which is why I think Steve was able to joke about it later in the locker room. But I just remember looking down and it seemed like Crowe had just enveloped Steve Thomas, who again was not a small guy. He just was on top of him and I remember thinking, 'Oh wow, this guy is going to get hurt right now.'

"So I came in after the game and at the Meadowlands the home team dressing room was really, it was just a room; it was a tight door to get through.

"And so basically, I was in this crowd of media, because there was a lot more media covering the Devils back then. It was a full house and I squeezed myself through the door. I immediately stepped to my right and I stepped on the stick blade of Chris Terreri's goalie stick. So I stepped on his goalie stick and this goalie stick, it was like a comedy routine because the stick slowly slid down against the wall and as it slid down, there was apparently one main light switch for the entire room, it turned the lights off as it fell. Mike Levine, who is standing by the door, caught the stick as he had seen the whole thing, looks at me and flips on the light because all the TV cameramen are staring at like, 'what happened to the lights?'

"He turns the lights back on, didn't say a word to me and puts the stick back. And I'm like, 'that's it. I'm never covering another hockey game again.' And so everyone gravitated to Steve's locker and I'm thinking, 'this guy's going to be pissed or he's going to be hurt.'

"And it was a great lesson for me about how hockey players think, because we went over to his locker stall and Stevie Thomas was just laughing his butt off about this. He was like, 'Oh yeah, Philly kicked my rear end.' He was like laughing about how hard the punches were and how much his face hurt. To me, if I got into a fight with someone I'm going to be pissed, especially if it gets to the point of physicality. In fact, I'd probably never talk to the guy again. But Stevie was talking about how maybe him and Phil would go out and grab some beers and chat. So I felt like I learned three things that day. One was to have an early story. Two was don't turn off the lights in the locker room and three was just how different covering hockey was.

"I've covered football. I've covered basketball. I've done a ton of baseball. I've done a lot of different sports. But hockey players, they're different. They don't take themselves too seriously. They're professionals, but they don't put themselves on that high horse that I think you see in other sports. You can relate to hockey players."

MOST UNFORGETTABLE DEVILS MOMENT

ANDREW GROSS: "In 2008, the Rangers and the Devils met in the first round of the playoffs. I think the Rangers won (the series) 4-1. What I remember is that it was a 5-on-3 power-play for the Rangers. (And I think the game was at The Garden, because the Rangers were wearing blue.) And so, you're following the puck around, which is what you normally do. And then I just remember Sean (Avery) is waving his stick back and forth in front of Marty's (Martin Brodeur) face. And I was riveted.

"I think, like everyone, I was just staring, watching Sean and I had gotten to know Sean a little bit and I'm like, 'well, this is totally in character right here.' Marty was pushing at him with his glove and Sean's not budging. Of course, the puck goes out of the zone and then it comes back in and Sean scores, I think it was (Scott) Gomez who set it up. And while he was pissed, Marty was the chillest dude ever.

"What I remember about Marty and this is even before getting on the beat, was you could talk to Marty 10 minutes before the game. I saw Rich Chere or Tom (Gulitti) at Madison Square Garden, when the teams used to come out through the tunnel, I'd see those guys chatting with Marty right before game time. Marty didn't care. He'd put on his mask and go play a game. He'd laugh at everything. But he wasn't laughing (at Avery's antics).

"And I forget whether I was the one who asked the question of Sean after the series was over after Game 5 -- Game 5 was at Prudential Center -- in the visiting room. We were talking to Sean and, of course, Marty did not shake Sean's hand on the handshake line. I think I asked Sean about it, and I apologize if it was some other reporter, and Sean's response was, 'I guess Fatso didn't want to shake my hand.' That series kind of stood out for that one play, because they changed the rule afterwards -- the Avery Rule.

"I was torn when it happened. I didn't think it was a very sportsman-like thing to do. But at the same time, the ugly part was that Sean was waving his stick in Marty's face and yelling stuff at him about Marty's divorce. And that's the thing most people didn't get. I was like, 'well Sean's being clever because it's within the rules. But I didn't think it was a sportsmanlike thing to do."

9 LARRY HIRSCH (NJ DEVILS RADIO)
THE EPIC COMEBACK VS. NEW YORK (@BRENDAN BYRNE ARENA)
NOVEMBER 2, 1985
NJD 6, NYR 5 (OT)

BACKGROUND

"Welcome fans, you're listening to New JERSEY Devils Hockey!" -- Larry Hirsch.

If you were a Devils fan at the beginning of the team's tenure in New Jersey, you knew this greeting well.

Every time a Devils fan turned on their radio to tune into the start of a Devils broadcast, they were greeted with Larry Hirsch's jubilant "hook." In fact, the greeting became so synonymous with Hirsch, that in later years, even after moving on from his role with New Jersey, he is still approached by fans (of all teams) and asked to do one more rendition of his famous "hook;" to which he happily obliges.

But how did this New York City native end up as the Voice of the New JERSEY Devils radio?

LARRY HIRSCH: "I did radio in college and loved it, passionately. I was going to be a politician. I was going to law school and I was going to be a public service figure. But I did radio in college and I fell in love with it. I said, 'how can you do this? I mean, I love to do it, but how am I going to make money? How am I going to do this?' And that flame and that thing I found that day, it stayed with me. When I went to law school, I met a guy who's a friend of mine, we grew up together. He did radio in college and we used to do interviews with other students in the hallway.

"Eventually, we got tickets to different games out in Los Angeles where we were: Rangers, Knicks, Celtics, Islanders and so on.

71

We took a tape recorder with us and did a game there. And it didn't sound too bad to me after we stopped laughing and went back home. But I said, 'Hey, that sounded pretty good.' So, on my own I took a tape recorder and did quite a few more games, culminating in a playoff game. I slept outside The Forum box office, with nobody around me, so I could get the first shot at the tickets so I could get the best location to do the game. And the difference was, the other games that I did, there were no people there, because they drew about 9,000 at that time. But they (the Kings) got good that year and made the playoffs for the first time in awhile.

"And so, consequently, I was going to be around people. I went ahead and I did it and the people enjoyed listening to me. I was very conscious of it. But anyway, eventually I went on to meet the voice of the Los Angeles Kings, Bob Miller. I talked with him and through him; I was able to get to Mike Hope, who was the Public Relations Director. He would give me a pass so I could go into the locker room, do interviews and that's how I culminated my first audition tape.

"My first job in radio was working for a Top-40 station where I learned the news, I learned writing the news, which is you having to compress everything into five minutes. Each story would get 30 seconds to 40 seconds with tape or whatever. I got my first break in hockey and broadcasting when I went to New Haven, Connecticut and I negotiated with the Athletic Director at Yale University. I said, 'I'll do games for you on radio.' And he said, 'no.' Now, I had a friend who had gone to Yale and when I went to see him once, we went to a hockey game and I thought it was unbelievable. So I said to the Athletic Director, "Well, I would like to do the games. What do you think about that?' And he said, 'Well, nobody's ever approached us to do the games before.'

"He wrote a letter, which compensated for legal and everything and it gave me the rights to Yale Hockey. How much did I pay? Zippo, nothing. I went to the best radio station in New Haven, which did Minor League Hockey as well. And I went to the Program Director and said, 'here's what I have in mind.' We talked about it and he said, 'okay, give me a three game schedule.' So I chose Cornell, Harvard and Princeton. The first game was against Cornell and Cornell was a big hockey club at that time. They were very good. And it was at 'The Whale' -- as they called it in Yale -- Arena. And then he said, 'how are we going to sell this?'

"So I said, 'Well, I'll sell it for you.' He said, 'Oh really? You can sell this?' I said, 'I'm going to sell it for you, because I can't do one without the other.' So I went out and I sold almost two-thirds of the broadcast. I went back to him and he was amazed, because his sales staff couldn't sell it.

"We were ready to do Game One. It was in the beginning of December. I was so pumped up and I got a call from the Program Director of WELI in New Haven and he says, 'Larry, we can't do the games.' I said, 'WHAT?' He was like, 'I got it from up top, there were some complaints, we can't do the games. We do the Minor League Hockey team, the New Haven Nighthawks and they weren't happy.' I said, 'you've gotta be kidding me. I got a commitment.' He said, 'you can't do the games. But here's the good news.' I said, 'there's good news?' He replied, 'Yeah, the color guy who does the games with our play-by-play guy, who is also our big morning guy, he's not working out and we don't like him. How would you like to do them?'

"And that was my first entry point. From there, they were the minor league team for the Minnesota North Stars and the St. Louis Blues, I went to Minnesota and I went to St Louis, traveled with my own money and met the PR people there. 'Hi, I'm Larry Hirsch from New Haven.'"

Eventually, Hirsch made enough contacts that he was able to move on to bigger and better gigs.

And one of the first places he went was Cleveland, where he was responsible for calling games for the Cleveland Barons of the NHL. (This was a short-lived gig as the Barons merged with the Minnesota North Stars after being in the league for only two years.)

However, Hirsch managed to land on his feet as he got a public relations and media consultant job in New York City. But that too didn't last long as Hirsch longed to go back to California. And eventually he did. And while out in California, another connection of his helped him land a job as a weekend sports anchor with KHJ Channel Nine at RKO Station television.

Then, thanks to his soon to be wife, Hirsch was put in contact with somebody who was friends with Dr. John McMullen, who had recently bought the Colorado Rockies and was moving them to New Jersey to be rebranded as the Devils.

LARRY HIRSCH: "I got an interview with John and one very, very hot Saturday afternoon I met him at his country club, The Montclair Country Club. He asked me who I thought the best announcers were in the NHL. And I said, 'Dan Kelly, Marv Albert and Bob Miller.' So he asked me, 'where do you fit in to this?' I said, 'well, I'm not a name but I'm going to make you a guarantee and if I don't come through, kick my butt out after one year.' He said, 'what's the guarantee?'

"I said, 'your team will be the number one rated team. Give me three years, your team will be the most listened to team on radio.' And then he asked me, 'how are you going to do that?' I said, 'that's what I do best.'

"Anyway, five days later he hired me and he didn't even have a radio station yet. This was in July and the team was starting in October. So, through a buddy of mine who eventually was my technician, I met a guy by the name of Herb Saltzman, who owned a radio station out in New Jersey. I asked him, 'Herb, what do you think? Would you like to do the Devils?' And he said, 'yeah, I'm interested.' Now, it wasn't a powerful one, but it was enough to get into New York and certainly in New Jersey.

"I put him and John McMullen together and they cut a deal. Within two weeks we had a radio station and then I just went to work. I became the Devils play-by-play guy. Before we did our first game, we had a press conference and Larry Brooks, who was our Public Relations Director in New Jersey at that time, knew Fred Shero. They both lived in Scarsdale. He got Fred to be the color guy and that's when I met Fred Shero, which was one of the greatest days in my life when I met him, because I learned 97% of my hockey from him.

"I was so happy to have him there and he didn't know anything about radio. But we got together like peas and carrots. Anyway, so that team was created and I crowned us as the 'Master Blaster' because of the way I did hockey and 'Dr. Hockey,' because Fred knew everything. We did everything to draw in audiences. We did a call-in show in-between periods called, 'Dial the Devils.'

"I'd run in General Managers, Coaches, people at the arena, to be my guest. I gave out the number for the purpose of getting callers to call-in and ask questions. It was all about fan participation. And through that we got names on a list and we handed the list over to the ticket department.

"It's God's honest truth. I'm not boasting. I'm proud of it. The promise I made to McMullen about how in three years we'd be Number One, well we were Number One after that first year, or right at the end of that first year. The ratings came out and we were the most listened to. I got fans involved."

MOST UNFORGETTABLE DEVILS GAME

From 1982-1987, New Jersey spent all of its time and energy trying to find a blueprint for success. But there was none to be had.

And in the midst of their stretch of futility was the 1985-86 season, one in which the Garden Staters lost a whopping 49 of their 80 games played.

However, there was one bright spot during their very trying season and that was a comeback win against their rivals, the New York Rangers.

The Devils entered the game with a 4-5-1, compared to the Blueshirts' 5-4-0 mark. And as the game got underway, there was no inkling that something special might happen for New Jersey.

New York's Mark Pavelich opened the scoring in the first period and his teammates, Mike Ridley and George McPhee, both added on to the Rangers' tally during the game. In fact, Pavelich himself netted a second goal during the middle period, as the Blueshirts built up a commanding 4-0 lead through just over 41 minutes of play.

However, New Jersey's Peter McNab wasn't willing to go down without a fight. And on the strength of his two-goals (one on the power-play), the Devils clawed back within 4-2 by the 7:11 mark of the third period.

Unfortunately, the Rangers' Mark Osborne took back control of the game by scoring a power-play goal of his own to give New York a 5-2 lead with just over eight minutes remaining in the game.

And that's when things got interesting.

LARRY HIRSCH: "The best game I was ever a part of was when the Devils beat the Rangers after losing 5-2. (The game took place on November 2, 1985). They were losing 5-2 in the third period after a power-play goal by the Rangers, with roughly eight minutes to go in the game. Then the Devils scored, it was 5-3. They scored again, 5-4. Now I'm saying, 'Hey, we can pull the goaltender.' And while I'm building this scenario, the coach of the Rangers, Ted Sator, did the most amazing thing.

"After we made it 5-4 he pulled his goalie, Terry Kleisinger and put in his second stringer, John Vanbiesbrouck to change the pace and slow the game down. Now, I'm saying on the radio. 'Shoot the puck. Spit the puck out. Do anything. Just get the puck and throw it on goal. This guy's been sitting for two-and-a-half-hours.' With 32 seconds left to go, Tim Higgins scores. Bingo, it's 5-5 and the place went nuts.

"In overtime, they dropped the puck and Peter McNab gave the puck to Mel Bridgman from the right circle. Bingo! 6-5, game over! At that point, I was in such a lather. I was at such a peak when I called the goal. Do you know where I ended up? I literally climbed up on the seat on the table in the Meadowlands press box, my hands were spread out. I was pumping my fist. I was standing up on the table and fans were looking at me. It was a moment of insanity, but it was one of those moments in hockey where you just let it all out.

"It was a crescendo that ended in the most dramatic form. That night, I went back home with my then Fiancée. I got into our apartment and I was watching the late news on CBS with sportscaster, Warner Wolf. And he's talking about the Devils' win and saying, 'Let's go to the videotape!'

"So they show the winning goal and then he says, 'and listen to that, the crowd's going crazy. But if you think the crowd's going crazy, you should see the Devils announcer.' They showed me up on the tables, my hands spread out and everything like that for everybody in New York to see that night. And he was the most watched sportscaster at that time.

"I'll never forget that night. I was expecting a call the next morning from the Devils saying, 'did you really do that?' But no call came. The fans loved it because you (I) became one of the fans, which is criticized by critics. But that's what the fans love."

MOST UNFORGETTABLE DEVILS MOMENT

LARRY HIRSCH: "This is, this is my signature story. I'm a person who, announcers in most towns are identified by the fans, not only through their announcing, but also by them coming up with a saying, a niche fans hook onto. Phil Rizzuto used to say, 'Oh My!' Marv Albert was, 'Yes!' People hook on to that. John McMullen hated the New York Rangers. He wanted nothing to do with the Rangers and he wanted his team to win. And if you mentioned the New York Rangers, you're fired. In New Jersey, he wanted to create his own thing. And he told me, 'Larry, I don't want to hear anything about the Rangers on your broadcasts.' 'Yes sir.'

"So I mentioned to my buddy Carl, one of the first couple of games we did. I said, 'when I go out, I want to say, you're listening to New Jersey Devils Hockey on WMCA.' But in the back of my mind, I said, 'don't say New York Rangers.' So I was doing this game and right at the beginning of the commercial break I said, 'We'll be back, Devils lead 1-0 and you're listening to New York...' And I caught myself. We went out and when we came back, I said to Carl, 'I'm never going to do that again.' How I did it was to emphasize the 'J' in Jersey, just to make sure it's going to be Jersey coming out of my mouth and not New York. So I said, 'you're listening to New Jersey Devils Hockey,' really banging the Jersey.

"Next thing I know, fans are coming up to me, not only in Jersey, but also the Islanders fans and the New York Rangers fans. That was the hook. The proof of the success of that was when we did the All-Star Game in New Jersey. I think it was 1984. I got the Devils to do the game locally (on radio), so I was doing the game. But we also hooked up with Armed Forces Radio and we were heard all around the world.

"Two wonderful things happened that night, aside from just doing the broadcast, which I loved. One, I got to introduce the home team, the Prince of Wales team. They had a dais I sat at on the ice. I walked out on a red carpet. Mike Emrick, who was the TV guy, introduced the away team, the Campbell Conference and I introduced the Prince of Wales Conference. But before hand, I was pacing backstage because I had an idea I wanted to do it, but I didn't want to embarrass him. I thought, 'what am I doing? A new idea in front of these thousands of fans. I've got Canada TV. I've got US TV. It's the All-Star Game. Why am I going to do this? Do this some other time.'

"What I did to verify the hook I created in New Jersey was, I went up to the podium and I said, 'welcome to the Hockey Taj Mahal of the world! The Meadowlands, Brendan Byrne Arena!' And they didn't like Brendan Byrne. The boos started a little bit and I said, 'and home of New Jersey Devils Hockey!'

"The fans just went nuts and it worked, I was able to introduce the team. The last person I introduced was, 'and in goal, Number One, from the New Jersey Devils, Glenn Chico Resch!' And I really let the 'Chico' out. The fans just went nuts because they loved Chico.

"Anyway, that was probably my biggest thrill."

10 MATT LOUGHLIN (NJ DEVILS RADIO, WFAN)
THE LINE BRAWL (@MADISON SQUARE GARDEN)
MARCH 19, 2012
NJD 2, NYR 4

BACKGROUND

Ever since the Devils came to New Jersey in the fall of 1982, there has been one constant. And that has been the presence of absolutely fantastic broadcasters, both on television and radio.

Names such as: Larry Hirsch, Mike "Doc" Emrick, Stan Fischler, Glenn "Chico" Resch, Steve Cangialosi and so many more, have populated the Devils' airwaves for going on 37 seasons.

And one name that has been around for close to 90% of the Devils stay in New Jersey is Matt Loughlin. Loughlin has been featured on Devils' television and radio for several decades now and he's still going strong as the 2019-2020 season approaches.

For Loughlin, it has been a dream come true to cover a professional sports team, in his home state, that actually embraces its' Jersey home. And he's had quite the impressive journey to get to where he is today.

MATT LOUGHLIN: "I went to Seton Hall University and the plan was to be an accountant. I loved math. Quick side note, I had a wonderful math teacher in high school and her name was Dorothy Holiday, she's since passed away; 'Dot' Holliday. And when I told her I was planning to go to Seton Hall to study accounting, she said, 'you'll hate it.' And I said, 'why?' She goes, 'it's not mathematics; it's arithmetic and then law. It's addition, subtraction, multiplication and division and then it's law. You're not going to like it.' Well, what does she know? So I went to Seton Hall, primed to be an accountant and she was absolutely right. I absolutely hated accounting, it was very boring. That being said, I wasn't going to get out of school in anything more than four years.

"But during that time, so now it's freshman year (1975), I really haven't started my real accounting courses and, of course, I was a big sports fan. I watched and listened to sports all my life, loved all the local teams. So I'm listening to my team, Seton Hall, the games were broadcast by the school's radio station, WSOU. And sometime during my freshman year, there was a notice in the school newspaper, 'Hey, if you want to be a part, we're always looking for people.' I never thought where it would lead, but I thought it sounded interesting. So, at the end of my freshman year, literally I finished my last exam of freshman year and I walked across campus from the business school, up the steps of Walsh Auditorium and into the radio station.

"I knocked on the door and asked how I could get involved. The incoming Sports Director for that following year was there along with the Station Manager, who was a faculty rep and they both welcomed me with open arms and said, 'listen, come on in, you're a student here. Whatever you do, whatever you put in, you'll get out. Work here a little bit, you'll get a little out of it. Work here a lot. You could potentially get a lot out.' And from that moment on I was just absolutely in love with the media and the radio. I walked in, the noise, the energy, it just felt like home.

"So anyway, I did finish with a business degree, but I switched from accounting to marketing because that following year when I started taking accounting courses I hated them. But I wasn't getting out in more than four years. So, I switched to marketing. Anyway, I just worked my way up. I just kept doing more and more at the radio station. And when I got out, I started to apply to a lot of places and I began working for a radio station in New Jersey, WCTC, it's in New Brunswick, near my home. While I was at Seton Hall, Bob Lee, ESPN, was working for a local cable company called Suburban Cablevision. He came by the radio station and said, 'listen, why don't you come?' And it was located in the next town over; the headquarters. He said, 'why don't you come over, I'll teach you some of the ins and outs of television and I can always use some free labor,' which is exactly what it was. So I started to do some television.

"A year after I graduated, I spent a year doing news and this company, Suburban Cablevision, has an opening in their sports department. Bob had left to go to ESPN and Bruce Beck became the Sports Director and he said, 'we have an opening. Do you want the job?' Then I got the job and I turned to TV. And then, I just started knocking on doors and eventually SportsChannel hired me and I started covering a lot of things; college football and college lacrosse to start. That was the regional network break that I got and then I just kind of progressed from there.

"It was the late-80's when I was starting to do a couple of events here and there for SportsChannel. As I said, it started with me doing Hofstra Lacrosse and Hofstra Football and I guess I passed whatever muster they had and I started filling in for Stan (Fischler). There were two sports channels, the main channel and the backup channel. They had the Nets, the Devils and the Islanders in the winter. There were many conflicts, so they had this overflow channel. So, whatever hockey team was on the main channel, Stan would do and there were two of us who were filling in for him. So when the Islanders were on the backup channel, Carl Reuter, a Long Island based journalist, would fill-in. When the Devils were on the backup channel, me being a Jersey Guy, I would fill-in.

"After a couple of years, I wound up getting hired to do it regardless, Islanders and Devils. And so that was really the beginning, filling in for Stan. And then it just parlayed as SportsChannel decided to increase its budget and wanted to up its ante a little bit. I just eventually worked that into a full-time job, but not with hockey. It became a full-time job with basketball, the New Jersey Nets. But I was still fill-in, going back and forth, but I was Nets, Nets, Nets. And then when there was an opening that matched an opening in my schedule, I would do a Devils event. But then in '96-'97, it became a full-time gig. I moved away from basketball and was doing Devils full-time."

That's a really incredible journey for the Jersey native. And his journey isn't complete just yet.

MATT LOUGHLIN: "This will be my 14th year, coming up, doing radio. What had happened was, 2004 was the lockout year and then I came back and did one year (2005-06) and then 2006-07 was my first year doing radio. I was doing all my stuff with the Devils, loved it, but I had also been doing the Mets as well. They then left to their own network and so I was just doing the Devils and I enjoyed it. It was great. The Devils were winning and they were a championship team. I was working with Doc Emrick and Stan Fischler. Roland Dratch, our producer, was an awesome guy to deal with. Just a lot of fun. I'm in my home state, the team wears the Jersey logo; all that sort of stuff was good.

"But, going back to when I got into the business, I really, I loved radio. I loved everything about it. I'm still more of a listener than a watcher. But, you follow whatever path you need to follow to get where you can. And it happened to be television. So this job opens up and I thought about it long and hard and a couple of people, including the guy, John Hennessy, who was let go, told me I should apply for it. He thought I'd be great. And it sat there. I always wanted to be the play-by-play guy and I wasn't getting much of an opportunity. It was nobody's fault. It just wasn't my role.

"SportsChannel morphed into Fox Sports Net and Fox Sports Net New York and then ultimately into MSG. But Doc Emrick was going nowhere. He's an Emmy Award winner. He's the best there's ever been. And he loved doing that gig. So there didn't seem to be anyway for me to get a play-by-play job. I was filling in for him when he would have national assignments, but I never was going to get the job. And I thought, 'you know what? This is really where I want to be.' I want to be the play-by-play guy.

"I had a family, three boys, two who were in high school, one who was in grammar school. I wasn't going to traipse them all over the country and my wife. I'd established family here. I'm from here. So I wasn't going to try to scratch that itch so to speak, by finding a job elsewhere. But here it came. A team I know. The team I'm covering. The team I'm working with and so, I applied for the job and I got it. And so now, 14 years later, I'm more radio guy than a TV guy."

MOST UNFORGETTABLE DEVILS GAME

The 2011-12 Devils were a team on a mission. That mission? To win a FOURTH Stanley Cup championship. But before New Jersey could earn its way into the Stanley Cup Final, it had to first earn its way into the playoffs.

And before the Garden Staters could earn their way into the playoffs, they had to first make it through the grueling marathon that is the NHL regular season.

Now, there are some games that stand out more than others when it comes to the regular season. Some games bring more electricity. Others act as vessels for historic achievements. And some even act as a prelude for things to come.

So, whenever the New Jersey Devils crossed the Hudson River to face their blood rivals, the New York Rangers, or the Blueshirts crossed into Newark, you could be damn sure that the fans in attendance would be treated to an experience they'd never forget. And, of course, that sentiment extends to the players, writers, broadcasters, etc. as well.

With an archive full of memorable games and moments between these two teams, you almost have to stop and ask yourself, "what more can these teams do to each other?"

Well, how about a good old fashion line brawl?

The date was March 19, 2012, and the Devils were getting ready to face the Rangers inside The World's Most Famous Arena. Little did they know what was about to occur. And for one Devils broadcaster, this game was going to be one he would take about for years to come.

MATT LOUGHLIN: "It was March 19, 2012, at Madison Square Garden and the Rangers were a first place team. The Devils were going to be a playoff team. And in a rough and tumble series, it was the sixth game of the regular season series, a line brawl breaks out at the start of the game. And it was just great. I loved it, not because I'm a man who supports physical violence, but in our game we still need to have that element and its slowly eroded to the point where it's almost nonexistent.

"But at that moment, that game, even though the Devils lost, spoke to me about the rivalry. There had been many fights in the five games previous, including another line brawl, which was only two guys involved; this was a full three. But the scene was incredible. Brandon Dubinsky, who had his nose broken earlier with the Rangers, had just recently returned. But because he's got a broken nose, still, he can't fight. He steps in to take the draw against Ryan Carter.

"And we find out later he said to Ryan Carter, 'good luck.' And he backs out. So now, Sherry Ross and I are sitting in our perch at The Garden getting ready for the game and it's just this roar at that moment, where those two teams, at that point in their seasons and what had transpired, it was just there, like there was a fire. And we know something's up because Stu Bickel had just come in to take the face-off.

"What is going on here? Well we kind of knew what was going on and it didn't take long. They dropped the puck and fights break out. It's three guys just pounding each other. The crowd is going crazy. John Tortorella was barking at Pete DeBoer and Pete DeBoer was barking back at John Tortorella. Ryan Carter wound up being taken down to the ice ultimately. He got in a couple of really good punches on Bickel, but they got taken down and wound up breaking his nose on the ice.

"Bryce Salvador came over to try to help him out and instead of being a third man in and being kicked out, the officials kind of looked around and said, 'well you were just really helping a teammate. There was a lot of blood. We were busy elsewhere.' They only gave him a 10-minute misconduct, but it just was fantastic. And in many ways it set the tone for that 2012 Eastern Conference Final, because there were so many memories. The institutional memory of the Devils-Rangers rivalry and all that had transpired previously in '94, even though it was 18 years ago, it was still there.

"They beat the Devils in the Conference Final and won their first Stanley Cup in so many years. The Devils never really were able to beat them enroute to a Cup. So it was like, when are you going to put 'Big Brother' in his place? And while that night didn't do it, it set in motion what happened two months later when the Devils went in and beat them in six games. And even though they didn't win a championship, to me, that exercised their demons."

Even for two teams who really didn't -- and still don't -- like each other, this was a night that really brought the rivalry up another notch or two. In fact, it kind of harkened back to the days of the Original Six, when line brawls were more commonplace and fights would spill into the stands. Now, that's not to say this was a regular occurrence, rather it was just something that happened from time to time when it was needed.

MATT LOUGHLIN: "There were 11 fights between the teams that year. This year (2018-19), the Devils as a team, all season long, had 15. So that was when the game still had that element of physical toughness that has eroded. The roar. The reaction afterward where Tortorella was pissed that Pete had put out his tough guys, his fourth-line at the start, but Tortorella had done it earlier at The Rock.

"And so, Pete came back with the classic line, 'Well, either he's got a short term memory issue or he's a liar.' So, to me, even though it didn't result in a Devils win, it spoke about hockey, the rivalry and the rawness of it. And I talk about it all the time, because you'll never see it again. And I'm not a violent guy. But I just think that's an element of the game we still need. And on that night, in that venue, the Devils stood up for themselves, even though they lost

"Well, you knew in the previous games there had been a lot of fights. Again, it was still a part of the game. You knew the Rangers were holding onto first place. The Devils were still clawing their way into a playoff spot. They were in a playoff spot. They didn't need the win so much, but certainly it would have helped. And they hadn't secured anything. So, going in, it was a chance for the Devils to reestablish themselves. That season series ended 3-2-1 in favor of the Rangers.

"So it was even going into that game. The Rangers wound up winning to take their third win. And you knew they could very well be on a collision course. So how was what was going to take place this night, going to impact any potential meeting down the road?

"And this was Marty Brodeur near the end of his career. This was (Ilya) Kovalchuk putting the previous year behind him, where Johnny Mack gets fired and Jacques Lemaire comes in. The Devils were somewhat of a mess the year before. Kovalchuk wasn't playing any kind of a team game. Lemaire was able to convince him, 'okay, well you can score 30 goals, but we need, just once in a while, for you to get back here.' And he bought into it. It was one last kick at the can for Petr Sykora who had comeback. The bank was reunited with Patrick Elias. So all of those things are there.

"David Clarkson was having a great year. Zach Parise, you knew the backdrop there. He was playing out his contract. He's the captain. He's the homegrown kid. He's that first round pick in 2003. Fan Favorite. Now he's in the last year of his contract. Is this the last we're going to see him play for the Devils? So there were so many things that went into that season. It was Pete DeBoer's first year. You knew something was going to happen, inevitably.

"Cam Janssen was going to fight. Eric Boultoon was going to fight. That's what those guys did. They brought that energy level. It was going to happen. Nobody knew it was going to happen, until warm-ups were over. Everybody skated off, we were waiting to get handed the lineup sheets and then we came back from a commercial and were ready to go. The Anthem had been played and low and behold -- we knew when the Anthem was being sung, who was out there -- I'm looking at Sherry going, 'we're going to see something now.' She was not as in favor of it as I was, which is fine, but I was like, 'here we go.'"

While Sherry's trepidation was understandable, this was -- and is -- the type of rivalry where the bad blood is not contained to just the ice. Of course, I'm not saying that the media or the fans are going to fight each other, far from it. (Well, maybe the fans will if they've been drinking). But there is always a palpable tension when rivals like the Rangers and Devils meet. Even the reporters who cover the teams get a little more jacked up than they usually would.

MATT LOUGHLIN: "This is hot. This is a rivalry. This is what it's all about, right here, at this moment. This puck gets dropped and they know what they're going to do. We know what's going to happen and the crowd was in a roar.

"Eventually, things did calm down a little bit. I mean, once that energy dissipated, it was not going to happen right away again. It was just too much energy that was used up in those first three seconds. So you knew now, okay, now let's play the game. But you have guys in the penalty box. Bryce Salvador, he's gone. So the Devils are really short-handed.

"One of their key defensemen was not available for 10 minutes. The Rangers took early control. And really, the Rangers, thinking back on that game, they were pretty much in control the whole way. After the game, Marty Brodeur wasn't too happy. Again, it was him and Lundqvist and that side story. But he was like, 'that's not what we came for. We came to win the game and we didn't win the game.' And I understand that, because that's what an athlete is doing. But, it's still, to me, is a night that I talk about.

"That being said, the Rangers kind of controlled things. The Devils never pushed them to the point where they were sending a message, 'when we meet, we've gained the toehold; we're the better team. We beat you up.' And you could argue that Carter having his nose broken, they won the battle. I think it was pretty much probably even. So there's no gain made by the Devils in the fight or the fights themselves. Again, the Rangers won. And it was kind of like they said, 'okay, you brought out your tough guys. You brought out the nuclear option. We went at it toe-to-toe and we came out with a victory and we won the season series and we're still the Rangers and you're still the Devils.

"So I do remember leaving that game, a combination of disappointed and pissed, because I am a fan, trying to be objective as I can be, but such a moment that it didn't work out where the Devils could leave the arena heads held high. And that's why the "Adam Henrique, it's over!" was even more special, because they hadn't gotten over the hill that night.

"And I do remember a sense from Cam and Eric that, 'well, we didn't win the game, but man, that was fun.' Especially for Cam Janssen, that to him, that's what hockey should be like. He could still find a way to play this game and stay in this game because of the element he brought. And they all were like, 'hey, nobody left. Nobody went for a hot dog. We know it was early in the game, of course. But they were all on their feet.'

"And you know, the Devils and Pete made a statement by putting those guys out there. He knew Tortorella had one of two responses. He could put out as top-line and try to take advantage of their skill against the Devils' ruggedness. Or he could take the bait, which he did, and say, 'you're not going to do that in my home rink. You think I'm not gonna take a chance. You might do something to our more skilled guys. So here we go, let's have at it.' And to the Rangers' credit they won. But it's still, just that roar, that feeling, that energy, it's something that won't happen again. And that's okay. It's okay in a way. But just to be part of that and around that was pretty cool."

MOST UNFORGETTABLE DEVILS MOMENT

MATT LOUGHLIN: "In 1995, I wasn't covering the team full-time. As I said, I had been filling in, but I was covering basketball. But now as the Devils went to the post-season SportsChannel said, 'we want to add to our coverage, so you'll be part of the team.' So, the Devils played Detroit, that whole run was just incredible. That was my first playoff experience in hockey and that's where I'm very good. So it was my first real experience covering winning sports at the professional level. At any rate, so we're in Detroit and I can't believe I'm there, because it wasn't until 1994, that I left my job that I had mentioned earlier, to see if I can make something happen here full-time.

"And so here I am, a little over a year later, in the Stanley Cup Final, amazed that I've made this transition from doing primarily high school sports to now I'm at the pinnacle, doing the Stanley Cup. The New Jersey Devils were playing a historic Original Six franchise for all the marbles. They were given no chance, no hope of winning. And then they won. But my moment is me speaking with Jim Dowd and I will never forget it. It was an off day in Detroit and I'm talking to Jimmy, we're both Jersey guys and I had covered him in high school. He's from South Jersey. I didn't cover him regularly, but I covered Brick when they went to the state championship. So there was some recognition there on his part, even though he didn't really know me by name. He had seen me during his senior year when they won.

"But then we made that connection there and I was like, 'Jimmy, two Jersey guys and we're here in the Stanley Cup Final and it's just incredible.' So I can see him sitting, leaning against the wall and me just talking to him. And it really wasn't Devils hockey at all. It wasn't Stanley Cup hockey. It was just two Jersey guys. So that's the moment that would stand out. I mean, the Devils hadn't clinched yet, they'd only won Game 1 and here we are, talking about two Jersey guys.

"Later in that series when the Devils won, as soon as the game was over, SportsChannel did a post-game show and I brought us on the air. I remember sitting in the corner of the Meadowlands, which is where our studio was. It was just like an area where handicap fans could sit. Well, there's a little opening where we set up a camera and it's over, the place is going crazy.

"The Devils have won the Stanley Cup. They've completed this unbelievable sweep and I'm bringing us on the air and it's kind of emotional. This is a team that takes the New Jersey name; they didn't want to be the New York Devils. They're the New Jersey Devils. They had won, a 4-0 upset. The noise was kind of resounding through the building and I was welcoming everybody onto the show. But before that, while the countdown's on and we're just about to come on, to see the people, the roar of the crowd, the players' sticks in the air, was just phenomenal.

"The picture I would take out of my career would be sitting in that little corner of the Meadowlands, the Devils' first championship, in June, the place is going crazy and I'm welcoming our viewers on the air and the Devils have won the first of three (Stanley Cups) and were on their way to becoming an elite team."

11 COREY MASISAK (THE ATHLETIC)
DEVILS 1ST GAME OUTSIDE NORTH AMERICA
(@POSTFINANCE ARENA)
OCTOBER 1, 2018
NJD 3, SC BERN 2 (OT) (PRE-SEASON)

BACKGROUND

The most important thing young sports writers should know is that they need to be prepared to move around quite a bit in the early stages of their careers. And if they're not willing to do that, then they need to look at a different profession.

Now, you might be asking why am I being so negative? The answer is, I'm really not. I'm just conveying that truth about a particular career path.

And a perfect example of a young sports writer who was prepared to do whatever it took to succeed, is the story of how Corey Masisak became the New Jersey Devils' beat writer for *The Athletic*.

COREY MASISAK: "So, I grew up in Pittsburgh and I was eight when they won The Cup for the first time. And so, I got into hockey pretty young. It wasn't quite me in diapers; that was baseball. But I was always into hockey. I went to the University of Maryland where I used to go to Caps games. My freshman and sophomore years, they had the top two levels around the arena, the top two rows, it was called the Eagle's Nest and you could get tickets for 10 bucks. So we would go to probably six or seven games a year that way. And actually, while I was still in college, I started working at the *Washington Times* and then basically dropped out when they offered me a full-time job.

"I was doing all sorts of things. I covered Navy football for a bit and I was the backup Nationals writer whenever the Nats first came to town. I even went to Redskins Training Camp one year. And then, the guy who was the Capitals writer, Dave Fay, who was the long-time Capitals beat writer, got cancer. He had had it before and then it came back. So I started covering the team in January of 2007, when they were terrible. And then, he got better in the summer, everything was okay and then he passed away late in the summer. So they made me the full-time beat writer for the next year, 2007-08. That was the first year that they made the playoffs.

"So I covered them until the *Washington Times* decided it didn't want to have a sports section anymore. They fired the entire staff, it was like 25 of us and we found out on Christmas Eve 2009. And New Year's Eve was our last day. So then, the rest of the 2009-10 season, I was basically a freelancer, pretty regularly, for a TV website. Back then it was *CSN Washington* and I guess now it's *NBC Sports* or whatever it's called. Anyway, I wrote for *CSN Washington*, wrote some stuff for *NHL.com* and whoever else would pay me. I spent the first half of the next season doing that. And then, in November, I was actually covering a Devils game that night and during the day I interviewed for a job at *NHL.com*. That night I wrote one of the more controversial or famous stories about the Caps while I was there.

"There was a thing that happened right outside the visiting locker room where Ilya Kovalchuk, Alex Ovechkin and Alexander Semin were all kind of yucking it up in the middle of Bruce Boudreau's press conference. The Caps had lost 5-0, just got their doors blown off and Bruce was really pissed. He was steaming and red in the face, like how he gets after the opposing team scores a goal. We saw it during that press conference. And so, right at the end of it, I was like, 'does that bother you?' And he sort of gave a noncommittal answer, but it was very clear and everybody knew what was going on. So the next morning, I wrote a story about that and then a few weeks later, I got a call from *NHL.com* and they offered me the job.

"I started working there in the middle of January 2011. It was right in the middle of January. I moved up to New York and was at *NHL.com* from January 2011 until the end of the 2015 playoffs.

"Then, to borrow a line from Goodwill Hunting, "I had to go see about a girl." I quit. I basically told them in the middle of the playoffs, 'I'm quitting at the end here.' My girlfriend at the time was living in South Florida and she got a job at the *Sporting News* in Charlotte. So I moved to Charlotte. I spent a few months drifting, not really doing a whole lot. I got a job at a college football website. And then she got a job at *NHL.com,* so we moved back to New York."

Talk about doing a complete 360! But I guess the heart wants what the heart wants.

COREY MASISAK: "I got a job at the *New York Post* working on their desk as an Internet writer/editor person. Digital Editor I think might be the right title. By then, *The Athletic* had started and I knew everybody who worked there on the hockey side and was pretty good friends with a lot of them. I had talked to them a little bit here and there about it. Like, 'Hey, is there anything in New York?' And for a long time it seemed like New York was at the bottom of the priority list. And then one day it just sort of happened. They were like, 'Hey, we're going to have a New York site.' They didn't hire me at first. They didn't have a Devils writer the day it launched.

"But literally, in the first two days, they got so many messages from people who were Devils fans asking, 'Where's the Devils writer?' So, on the third day of the site, they called me and said, 'Hey, would you like to come and cover the Devils?' And within a few days I had accepted the job. I started; I think my first official day was March 14, 2018. I started hanging around the team when they had a road trip to like Nashville, Vegas and somebody else I think. I started introducing myself to people before that road trip. And then after they came back I started working on stories full-time."

It's only been a little over a year-and-a-half, but Masisak has adjusted quite well to the Devils beat and is now one of the "Go To" writers who cover the team.

MOST UNFORGETTABLE DEVILS GAME

When a team that has been around for several decades gets to do a "first," it's something special. And it's not just special for the team, but also for the players, coaches, writers, broadcasters, fans, etc.

So, when the Devils took a trip to Switzerland in late-September/Early-October of 2018 to conclude their pre-season slate of games, it was special. And even more so because it meant that Nico Hischier would get to play in front of his native countrymen and countrywomen while representing the Devils and the NHL.

Now, normally, asking a sophomore player to be the face of an international event would be cause for some concern. But Hischier handled everything beautifully. And given how he was raised, that's really no surprise. But first, before any NHL games were played on the ice, the Devils were scheduled for an exhibition match against Hischier's former team, SC Bern, with the game set to be played at the historic PostFinance Arena in Bern, Switzerland.

And being that this game would be the first New Jersey Devils game ever played outside North America, who was there to cover such a momentous occasion? How about Corey Masisak.

COREY MASISAK: "It was a once in a lifetime kind of thing. I mean, *The Athletic* had been around for I believe three years at that point. When I sat down with my boss during the summer, we talked about things to do for the season and the first thing was the Devils' trip to Europe.

"So, I put together my plan and what it would cost and the next day they were like, 'let's do that.' It was just incredible. The Devils played a pre-season game at The Garden and that was the day I left for Switzerland. They then went to Winnipeg and then made their way to Bern, which is where I met up with them. But before that, I went to Nico Hischier's hometown in Naters, Switzerland. I flew into Zurich and got there around dinnertime. So then, I had to drive to Nico's hometown in the dark, which was like a three-hour drive. And one of the very first lessons I learned was that there were trains that went through the mountains. So I drove my car up onto the train and went through the mountain.

"Well, turns out, the one I wanted to take to Naters didn't run after like Six O'clock. I was sitting there for like half-an-hour when somebody came up to me and told me that. So I was like, 'Shit, what do I do?' So the person said to me, 'oh, you can drive over the mountain.' I was like, 'okay.' So I drove on this one lane road, up and around the mountain, which was an interesting experience. As a side note, I don't own a car here in The States, so whenever I have to do any sort of weird driving, I get a little antsy.

"Eventually, I got to my destination and I met with Nico's parents. I basically spent three days in that area. I went to their house, had lunch and really got to know them. It was one of the most beautiful places I'd ever seen. They live halfway up the mountain and when you look out from the terrace, you can't even imagine what the view is like."

As a side note, Corey showed me some photographs that he took from the Hischier's home and they are exquisite. The views he talks about, they're really unbelievable.

COREY MASISAK: "I think the best way to describe his family is that they are what we think of as the ideal American family. They are the All-American family, just in Switzerland. His dad was a professional soccer player. His mom was a swimmer. All three of their kids are great athletes. Two of them are professional hockey players and their daughter is a very good volleyball player. And they're all really nice people. They were just incredible. They welcomed me in and his mom had some different meats, cheeses and desserts set up.

"It was just a very unique interview experience. And, obviously, one of Nico's defining characteristics is that he's just a normal, humble guy. And it's very obvious he gets that from his parents. His dad played professional soccer and now sells insurance. He was never like a hockey dad, or one of those parents who would complain, 'why isn't my son playing?'

"He told me, 'we would have been happy if Nico played soccer or whatever sport he wanted to. But the fact he played hockey, I didn't really know a lot about the tactics and strategies, so that was probably a good thing.

"They were very hands off but they also taught him to work hard, do his homework and stuff like that. I even met with his youth coach down in Vista, which was like two towns over. He took me to the old arena where they played. It was like this old barn with wooden slats on the roof and it was probably 20 degrees in there, even though it was probably 70 outside. But, maybe because of Nico, they were building a new, nicer arena for the local hockey club.

"So then, after meeting with everybody, I went to Bern and met up with the Devils. They got off the plane and they were just gassed. They looked like a bunch of zombies thanks to jetlag. But they came straight to the arena and Nico, along with Mirco Mueller, did 20 minute interview sessions with the Swiss media who were there.

"The Devils were getting ready to play SC Bern, who Nico had played for when he turned pro when he was like 15. His old coach had told me that there was almost a bidding war for Nico when he was 15, because everybody knew he was going to be the best player Switzerland had ever seen. And Nico chose Bern even though they didn't offer the most money. His aunt lived in Bern and his sister was going to college in Bern, so it just made sense from the family ties perspective.

"So, the next day, the Devils practiced. And one of the cool parts of the trip was that the Bern's arena was one of the most distinctive ones in Europe. One side of it is this giant wall that's like all bleachers. It looks like a soccer stadium would with all the flags and everything. And one of the things is that SC Bern has like the top attendance every year, so we knew it was going to be a pretty crazy environment.

"That night, SC Bern played their local rival EHC Biel and a bunch of the Devils players went to that game, as did I. It was like watching a European soccer game, with the two fan bases chanting back and forth at each other.

"So, the next morning, everyone was like, 'Oh my God, that was the most amazing experience I've ever had at a hockey game!' And now they were really stoked to play that night.

"Now, getting into the game, when the Public Address Announcer would say the first name of each of SC Bern's players, 'The Wall' would then shout the player's last name. So then, the Public Address Announcer went through the Devils starting lineup and held Nico until the end. And when he finally said Nico's name, the whole crowd shouted 'HISCHIER!' It was amazing! That alone would have been amazing and I'm pretty certain he was ready for it. But I don't know that his teammates were.

"They cheered and then 'The Wall' did a chant specifically for Nico, sort of like a song. And I'm pretty sure from his reaction that he wasn't ready for that. He played only a handful of games for them when he was like 15, 16-years-old. So that was probably his first experience with having 17,000 people chanting his name like that. He was pretty emotional and it was just an amazing way to start things off.

"From there it was a pretty close game, which the Devils ended up winning 3-2 in overtime when Taylor Hall scored with just 1:03 left in the extra period. And I know some people were surprised at how close of a game it was. But SC Bern was literally the best team in Switzerland. They actually won the Swiss championship that year. They had three or four guys who played at a pretty high level. And they played a pretty defensive style game. Plus, they played on Olympic sized ice and it was sort of like the Devils were trying to get adjusted to that. I mean, the Devils scored first, but it wasn't like they were able to pull away. It was a one-goal game the whole way through."

When Captain Andy Greene scored the first goal of the game, it was historic because it was the first Devils' goal ever scored overseas. And then, in the second period, Ben Lovejoy added to New Jersey's overseas tally when his slap shot gave the Devils a 2-1 lead.

COREY MASISAK: "And after the game, it was a different experience too. Everybody was just so happy to have taken part in something like this. I mean, John Hynes ripped into them in the second period because they weren't playing well after playing fairly well in the first. But overall, they all were glad to have taken part in it. And Nico was just struggling to come up with the words to describe what it was like for him. He had played a bit nervous throughout the game, but he had a couple really good chances where he just couldn't quite finish. But all in all, it was an interesting experience."

MOST UNFORGETTABLE DEVILS MOMENT

MASISAK: ""It's probably the view from the Hischier family's terrace. Part of the deal with working at *The Athletic* is that you get to do stories you wouldn't get to do anywhere else. I mean, I did get to do some of this stuff at *NHL.com* to a certain extent. Mike Morreale also took half-a-day and went down to meet the (Hischier) family and all that stuff too. But, just the totality of that experience was unlike anything I'd ever done as a journalist before.

"I was just sitting there with them and looking out and being like, 'How did I get here?' The view from where I stayed, basically I got an airbnb and then I got some local fresh bread and I sat out there in the morning and was just like, 'Holy shit, where am I?' So, I drove over to meet them and the really cool thing is, sitting there and looking down (from the Hischier family terrace) you can see the stadium where Rino, his dad, played and you can just look down into it. His, (Nico Hischier's), grandparents and his parents, the whole family has been in that town forever, or rather, multiple generations.

"I was just driving around to different towns, trying to come up with some scenic stuff to write about. Like, if I saw a kid walking down the street with a Nico Jersey on, maybe I would talk to them. So, there was basically one real sports bar in their town and another one that was pretty much just a bar, but they had a Nico jersey hung up. So I went into the sports bar and they had a whole shrine to Nico, all cool, old stuff all over the walls.

"You could tell this was the place to go. And in the back room there's a team photo from the 1995 or 1996, season of the FC Naters, the team Rino (Hischier) would have played for. But there were no names. It was just the players. And so I was like, 'man, I wonder if he's in this photo, because it was about the right time for when he would have been playing for them.' And there were three guys sitting there, if you could picture in your mind, you're at a European sports bar at two in the afternoon on a weekday. What would the three guys look like? And they were sitting there, one looking like he hasn't shaved in three days. One looked like he hadn't been to the gym in three years. And they were all in tracksuits. So I looked at them and I think one spoke English well, one was so-so and the other not at all.

"So I spoke to them and I asked, 'is Rino Hischier in this photo.' And so, they started looking at it and they named almost every guy in that photo. This was a third division team in Swiss soccer from roughly 20 years ago and these three guys, who were just sitting there, can basically name everybody on that team. I mean, it'd be one thing if you went to a bar in London and somebody named all the guys from

Arsenal's team in 1995; people can do that. But just to be in this little town, in this little bar and have those three guys just rattle off all the names of all these players, who are probably just shopkeepers and businessmen now, it was just remarkable."

12 MIKE MORREALE (NHL.COM)
"MARTY BRODEUR IS THE WINNINGEST GOALTENDER IN THE NHL!" WIN NO. 552!
(@PRUDENTIAL CENTER)
MARCH 17, 2009
NJD 3, CHI 2

BACKGROUND

If you are a Devils fan who likes to read anything and everything about the team, then you are probably familiar with Mike Morreale's work. From Morreale's elite game coverage to his uncanny knack for getting the best stories possible out of Devils -- and NHL -- prospects, Morreale is one of this generations' "must-read" writers.

And in case that isn't enough, Morreale is also a New Jersey native, so you have a hometown guy covering the hometown team. What could be more perfect? Okay, in fairness, perhaps it could be more perfect if he was actually a Devils fan growing up, for you see, Morreale rooted for the Philadelphia Flyers as a child. (Please put the pitchforks down, it's not like he grew up rooting for the Rangers). Besides, he eventually saw the light and came over to the Devils, so in my book (no pun intended) he's A-OK.

MIKE MORREALE: "I was always a sports fan growing up. As a youngster, my father and I used to play a lot of air hockey, we had an air hockey and a Nok-Hockey table and we'd always have tournaments.

"I actually grew up a big-time Flyers fan. I liked the demeanor of the 'Broad Street Bullies' and what they brought to the table. I kind of liked that rock 'em sock 'em style of hockey at that time. That's what interested me most about the game. And while I also enjoyed football, I just thought there was something about hockey players being on skates and being able to do incredible things at high-speed. And then, to also add the element of every so often having a player drop his gloves and have a little bit of a boxing match out there on the ice. I always found that fascinating and the Flyers were the best of the best when I was growing up watching them.

"So that's how I really picked up the game of hockey. (As for becoming a writer), when I was going to school, English was always my strong suit. I was horrible at math, although, now I have to really dive into analytics and stuff, so I'm learning. But I'm still old school in that regard. But getting back to English. I always enjoyed English. I enjoyed the term papers, as much as that may pain some fans out there. But I enjoyed thinking on my own and trying to come to a solution to problems and writing it down on paper. And then, when I went to college, I majored in journalism.

"I was really geared up to write for a sports newspaper at one point in my career. That's what I wanted to do. There were times in High School where, since I was always a big fan of the Flyers, I would try to get the Flyers' games on my little transmitter radio. And I lived in Jersey. So, if I held it a certain way on my bed, with twisting it a certain way, I was able to get Flyers games.

"I was so dedicated to listening to what the Flyers were doing, regular season or playoffs. And I was even more determined, because we didn't get Flyers games in the Metropolitan area, so I had to figure out another way to get them. I would listen to the games under my pillows so my mom and dad wouldn't hear the radio, because I knew it was a school day the next day. I didn't want them to come in and say, 'what are you doing?'

"So, when I was listening to the games, I was able to listen to different sportscasters. I remember, Dan Kelly was my favorite, aside from Gene Hart of the Flyers. I tried to emulate Doc Emrick, on the television side of things, the way he called hockey games. So I would set up my tape recorder and I would write down certain plays or certain things that happened and then I'd watch a game and try to mimic exactly the call they made. I would say it into a tape recorder and do it over and over again.

"I enjoyed the sportscaster side of it. But as it turned out, I enrolled at Rider College in Lawrenceville, New Jersey, as a journalism major. No minor, just the journalism major. I was all geared towards writing. I was a Sports Director for the radio station and an Assistant Sports Editor for the *Rider News*, which I did for all four years I was there.

"I covered all the sports there, as every young journalist does. You've got to start from the bottom and work your way up. So, after college, I was given an opportunity with *Dorf Feature Service* in Mountainside, New Jersey. What they offered was all the high school content for the *Star-Ledger*. The *Star-Ledger* would subcontract out to *Dorf Feature Service* to do all that work, in addition to other things, like, death notices, obituaries and horse racing results."

When Morreale graduated, he was primed to blaze a path of glory with a pen and pad. And that path started at *Dorf Feature Service.*

MIKE MORREALE: "I got the job when I graduated from Rider College in June of 1990 and immediately, I was brought on that summer to begin writing. And when I started out, the Chief Editor and Owner of the company, Gary Dorfman, brought me into his office and said to me, 'what do you want to do?' So I said, 'Well, I really enjoy hockey, but I'll do any sport and work my way up the ladder for as long as it takes.' So he told me, 'Well, this is what I'm going to do for you. You're going to start in the Obit department, because, if you can write an obituary, you can write anything. Obituaries are the hardest thing to write. The calls you have to make. The work you have to put into it. So, I'm going to put you there for a month and we'll see how you do. And then we'll think about sports.'

"So I did that for a month and I also did horse racing results. And at that time, I had no knowledge of horse racing. Basically, I was just like a Secretary. As the results came in from Aqueduct, or wherever it might be, I'd have to type in the results that you would see in the *Star-Ledger.*

"Eventually, I moved onto high school football, tennis, wrestling, all those sports. I even got into high school hockey a bit. And eventually, the gentleman who was covering high school hockey, left for another job. So, I was promoted to the Lead Writer for High School Hockey in New Jersey. That was around 1992 and from that point on, I started to establish myself as a credible source in high school hockey in New Jersey; which I absolutely loved.

"At the time, there were maybe 50 to 60 high school programs in the state. And I'm happy to say that today; there are over 120 high schools that have hockey programs. It's been an unbelievable ride for high school hockey along the way.

"I loved going to the rinks. I was there when James van Riemsdyk was a little freshman at Christian Brothers Academy. I was there when Kyle Palmieri was a little freshman at St. Peter's Prep in Jersey City. All the guys gave me their time whenever I needed to reach out for the All-State Teams or for the All-Century Team, on which, Jim

Dowd was my All-Century Player. When we put that together in 2000, they were all very accommodating when I needed to approach them after games.

"I spent 17 years at the *Star-Ledger* and I think that sent me in the right direction when I finally applied to the National Hockey League and *NHL.com*. And in January 2008, I began working at *NHL.com*. Of course, my parents played a huge role in what I'm doing today. They instilled in me a sense of pride and work ethic that I always try to maintain."

And along Morreale's journey, he has received numerous accolades for his work with high school hockey and for his overall coverage of the game we all love.

MIKE MORREALE: "Now, I've been doing Devils games for 11 years. Plus, I'm also the lead writer for the NHL Draft and prospect coverage. And that's almost like taking me back to when I was doing high school hockey, which is where it all began for me. Just learning about their personal lives, both on and off the ice, and to see how exceptionally talented some players are.

"It's just so nice. Even when I see James van Riemsdyk in an NHL locker room, he still calls me, Mr. Morreale. And I'm like to him, 'James, you're making a lot more money than me and you're a lot more popular. You can call me Mike.' I owe a lot to New Jersey High School Hockey and to where I am now with covering the Devils."

MOST UNFORGETTABLE DEVILS GAME

They say, "records are meant to be broken." And yet, every time a record is about to fall, there is a big commotion made regarding the Who, What, Where, When, Why and How of the matter.

Well, in hockey, just like in any sport, there are certain records that are considered sacred. Probably the most sacred is Wayne Gretzky's career points record of 2,857. And while it would take an absolutely extraordinary effort to topple "The Great One's" mark, there are several other records that are held in deep regard that are achievable under the right circumstances.

One such mark was Patrick Roy's career wins record of 551. However, long before Roy's illustrious career came to a close, a challenger emerged that would one day threaten his most cherished record. And that challenger was Devils netminder, Martin Brodeur.

At the time of Roy's retirement, (he hung up his skates following the 2002-03 season), Brodeur was more than halfway to the record, having claimed 365 wins over his first 10 seasons. And that left Brodeur just 186 victories shy of Roy's hallowed mark.

So, as Roy moved on from playing the game he loved, Brodeur marched forwards, steadily climbing the ladder to his place amongst the Pantheon of All-Time great goaltenders. And come the 2008-09 season, Brodeur was within arms reach of the top of the NHL Goaltenders' Mount Olympus.

What once seemed a fallacy was now about to become a reality, that is, until fate intervened. Brodeur went down in November with an elbow injury and would not return to the Devils until February 26, 2009; an absence of roughly three-and-a-half months.

Now just seven wins from the record, Brodeur got hot and recorded six wins in seven starts to pull within one victory of his idol's mark. And in Montreal, in front of Roy and the Montreal Faithful, Brodeur pulled into a tie atop the wins list by leading the Devils to a 3-1 win over the Canadiens.

Marty had secured at least part of the record and he only needed one win to call it his own. Could he do so in front of the Devils Faithful?

Mike Morreale was there to chronicle the historic game.

MIKE MORREALE: "It was March 17, 2009, and the Chicago Blackhawks were coming to New Jersey. (It was also St. Patty's Day in The States). When I first got to the arena, my job at that time was to kind of blog everything that transpired over the course of that day.

"I remember talking to Doc Emrick and asking him about his favorite Marty moments and did he feel Marty was the best goaltender ever? So he told me some of his Marty stories that I was able to use in my piece that day. And I just remember, the anticipation and the crowd filtering into the arena. I was having dinner with my colleagues, Dan Rosen and Shawn Roarke, who was our Managing Editor. Dan was our Senior Writer. The three of us were covering the game and we were going over the game plan on what I needed to do prior to the game and during the game. And when we were having dinner, I remember there being a lot of excitement in the media area.

"Even the Chicago Blackhawks broadcasters were excited about what might transpire. I remember going into both locker rooms and Joel Quenneville, who was the Chicago coach at the time, had a smile on his face as he was talking about Marty and how difficult he was to play against. Everyone had good things to say. They all knew something special could happen, but on the Chicago side, they were just hoping it wouldn't be that night.

"And I remember, in the Devils' room, Jamie Langenbrunner, who was the captain, telling us how great it would be to be on the ice to see Marty get the record. And Patrick Elias actually set the franchise scoring record that night as well. He was telling us how special it would be for (Marty to break the record) because they had won a Cup together.

"I remember, the Devils took the pressure off Marty by scoring three goals, two in the first period, including a goal by Jamie Langenbrunner 38 seconds into the game. And as the captain, Langenbrunner was jacked up to get that out of the way early. Then Travis Zajac scored at 6:01 of the first to give the Devils a 2-0 lead."

The Devils' third goal, at 16:56 of the second period, was the record-breaker for Elias, whose assist on the play gave him the most points in franchise history.

MIKE MORREALE: "I think everyone was hoping he (Brodeur) would get a shutout in the game. But that didn't happen."

The Blackhawks ended that possibility when Cam Barker scored a power-play goal at the 17:28 mark of the second period. And Chicago added another goal; this one from Dustin Byfuglien, at the 17:57 mark of the third period to ensure the last few moments of the game would be tense ones for New Jersey.

MIKE MORREALE: "I remember Brodeur making a pad save on Troy Brouwer in the waning seconds of the game and then jumping into the air once time had expired, and the fans were going crazy. It was a special moment. And the statue at the arena of him, where he's holding the stick in the air, that's from that day. It was just such an iconic pose.

"And then I remember him getting a pair of scissors to cut down the net, but he had trouble doing so. So one of his teammates went over to him and told him to take a victory lap.

"Anyway, after the game, he sat there for like 45 minutes to an hour making sure every question was answered, no matter who was late getting to the interview. That was another thing I always admired about Marty and I think it made you want to make the stories that much more special for a player like him when he was so willing to give you the time of day and to work with you in every way.

"And after we got everything and put our stories together, I remember Commissioner Gary Bettman saying, 'it's difficult to imagine any player who is more universally and deservedly respected than Martin Brodeur.' And I agree.

"So, in one game, two New Jersey Devils icons, two players who will forever be remembered by Devils fans as two of the best ever, set two remarkable records. And I was there on press row, a kid who used to listen to Flyers hockey games on a transistor radio under his pillow. And I've grown to become a Devils fan."

MOST UNFORGETTABLE DEVILS MOMENT

MORREALE: "I will never forget (when Brian Boyle scored his first goal after returning from cancer). It wasn't so much the result, as the Devils lost to Edmonton. It was November 9, 2017; 51 days after Boyle had been diagnosed with leukemia. For him to come on the ice, he was playing his fifth game after the diagnosis on September 19th and he scored a goal 5:33 into the first period, off a rebound to give the Devils a 1-0 lead. (It ended up being a 3-2 overtime loss against the Oilers.) You could just see the emotion on Boyle's face after he scored that goal. And I remember watching the replays on MSG Network. It just seemed like such a relief for Brian Boyle to get that goal and for his teammates, who were mobbing him and how appreciative they were.

"It proved that he was on the team and that he could score big goals and proved to everyone out there that he could play the game. And that he could work through his illness. He was getting better and better and he was willing to get on the ice with the Devils and show the world that he was still an exceptional hockey player, a guy who could play that two-way style and could compete with the other team's face-off guy. He was so emotional. I remember him scoring and then going into the right hand corner and kind of spinning around on the glass. I remember the fans along the glass were pounding the glass. And again, it was like a moment in time where it just kind of stood still, because you were just watching this and thinking, 'how in the world does a guy like this comeback from such a horrible disease and play so well and score that goal?'

"And then I remember, his between periods interview with Deb Placey on MSG Network and how he held it together. You could tell there was such emotion there. He was just about ready to start getting a little emotional, but he held it together about how appreciative he was of his teammates, Ray Shero and the ownership of the Devils giving him an opportunity to play on their team. He spoke about the doctors who played such a huge role in helping him get back onto the ice. His wife. His children. It was just a very emotional thing. And I remember, post-game, going into the locker room and he kind of just broke down and he started to let go a lot of the emotion that was inside of him.

"I'll just never forget him crying when he scored that goal. And, of course, he won the Masterton Trophy as the comeback player for that season. The quotes he gave me were, 'I'm not here if not for my wife and my family and my teammates. It's a little bit bigger tonight than probably ever.' So yeah, he was emotional. And those are the stories that really capture the heartstrings.

"I mean, you can have big time stories of teams winning Cups or a player setting a milestone. But when you get a story of a guy who was drafted and wasn't considered to be much of a player after he was drafted and then kind of works his way up the ladder and had to fight for every inch of ice time. And then he was stricken with a disease and he came back so strong and to do what he did, I thought it was quite a moment.

"And my other moment was on February 22, 2018, when the Minnesota Wild were coming to visit the New Jersey Devils. My daughter, who, she's now a graduate of Muhlenberg College, with a degree in theater and elementary education. She had asked me early in the summer, if the Devils had any auditions for people to sing the national anthem? And I said, 'yeah, I can call and find out when the auditions are.' They were in late August. I remember her going over there, I didn't go with her, but she said she did well enough where they said, 'we'll hook you up with a game. The game will be in February and we'll see how things go.' So I just remember the entire day of the game, her being so nervous and me trying to calm her down. But as a Dad, I was equally as nervous as she was. And I was covering the game.

"I felt like, here I am, a sports writer, with an opportunity to cover the game that my daughter would be singing the anthem at. It was really special and I invited all my family, some of my good friends, etc. And they all attended the game and we were cheering her on. She was nervous as heck. I mean we got there early, I drove her in and they did a quick little rehearsal an hour-and-a-half, two hours before the game. She said she was okay and they gave her a Devils jersey to wear that night, which she was really excited about.

"Now, my daughter really knows nothing about hockey. I never forced her to learn hockey. She'd ask me questions when we'd watch games of course. And if she wanted to know about the players, I'd answer them. But I'm not there to force hockey on her if she's not interested in it. But that day she was. She was asking me about certain players who were walking over to her and saying, 'good luck.' She had her own dressing room, which she was really excited about.

"Then when she came out, we were all in the stands. I didn't go on the press row to watch her sing the anthem. I went with my family and I just remember her doing a fantastic job and then going upstairs to start writing about the game. I knew where we were sitting as a family and she came down and I saw her get into her seat and she looked and turned around, she knew where I was in press row. She waved to me and I waved back to her. I gave her the thumbs up. We took all kinds of pictures.

"I remember Leo Scaglione Jr. took a nice picture and forwarded that picture to me. The people at Prudential Center got the video of the whole thing. I went into the Devils' locker room and I remember Andy Greene and Damon Severson asking me if that was my daughter who sang the anthem? And I was like, 'yeah, she did such a nice job.' I remember just feeling so proud of her. She got her one shot and she did a fantastic job. It's really a moment that I'll never forget. I mean, to have your daughter sing the national anthem at a hockey game, it was just something I never thought I'd ever see happen. Even John Hynes, prior to getting into the post-game media scrum, looked at me and said, 'Mike, by the way, your daughter did a real nice job with the anthem.' And that made me feel really good too."

13 DEB PLACEY (MSG NETWORKS)
"THEY SCORE! HENRIQUE! IT'S OVER!" (@PRUDENTIAL
CENTER)
MAY 25, 2012
NJD 3, NYR 2 (OT)

BACKGROUND

For 37 seasons, the New Jersey Devils have been blessed with terrific broadcasters, both on radio and on television. But there's more to broadcasting than just play-by-play and color commentary. There's also the task of hosting the pre- and post-game shows and the intermission reports.

And it was in the area of the pre- and post-game shows, along with the intermission reports, that the Devils always seemed to have a "knock it out of the park" type reporter. Specifically, from 2011-2018, Deb Placey was the Do-It-All-Host for MSG Network's Devils telecasts.

Placey's on-air presence, coupled with her vast knowledge of hockey and her outstanding chemistry with her colleagues combined to make New Jersey's broadcasts a must-watch show.

But how did Placey end up in this role?

DEB PLACEY: "I grew up in St. Louis, loving sports. I always wanted to be a journalist. And I always wanted to get into the field. I was fascinated by current events. Even as a kid, I was always reading the newspaper. I watched Tom Brokaw on the nightly news. I watched, if you remember as a kid, instead of cartoons on Saturday and Sunday morning, I was watching as they always had these kids doing the news where the globe would spin. But I was always fascinated by it and I guess I wrote during my time in elementary school, 'when I grow up, I

105

want to be a broadcast journalist.' So, I guess from the earliest age I knew that that's what I wanted to do.

"But I guess in my mind I always was going to be a news reporter. And so, I went to college and to Arizona to study journalism. And when I was there, a professor said to me, 'you know, if you know sports and you like it, sports is such an avenue right now for women. A lot of these local news directors are looking for sportscasters who are women.' There were very, very few women doing it at the time. Gayle Gardner had done some stuff for NBC.

"There were just very, very few women who had done it. Now, almost every young girl I talk to wants to be the next Erin Andrews. Everybody wants to be a sideline reporter or wants to get into the business. But back then, there were very few women doing it. So I took his advice and I tried to get an on-air job right out of college. But I was too young looking and too young to get hired on the air. But I did get a PA job at ESPN; they hired me to be a PA for SportsCenter. They put me in a program where after six-months you either stayed or left. It was a very competitive program.

"It was 1988 and after six-months I stayed. I was into my second year there when I got a call from a news director that I had applied with for an on the air job, two years earlier and said she had an opening in Marion, Illinois. It was a really small town in southern Illinois where Pete Rose had just gone to prison. John Gotti was there too, in the Marion Federal Penitentiary. And that was the town's claim to fame. She said, 'if you do news for me five days a week, I'll let you fill it on sports. So I packed up and moved myself across the country, by myself, to Marion, Illinois. I left ESPN. It was very hard to leave. They were very generous and even tried to get me to stay. But it would have been a straight, sort of up the ladder, promotion to become a producer."

Anybody who has had the pleasure of getting to know Placey, knows that she was -- and still is -- one of the most driven people in the industry. So there was no doubt she was going to chase her dream of being on-air.

DEB PLACEY: "And I thought, 'If I wanted to be on the air, then that was my time to try.' I did the news five days a week. It was a tremendous learning experience. I covered everything from City Hall, to local murders, of which there unfortunately were a couple. I also covered local politics, fluff stories and everything in between. So then, the weekend Sportscaster was getting married and I got to fill-in for two straight weekends. One weekend was for his wedding and the other his honeymoon. And then I sent out a tape and I got my next job in Providence, Rhode Island.

"Then, my next job after that was in Miami. And then, ESPN offered me a chance to come back to be an original anchor on ESPN 2. So I did that. Then my husband and I got married, we had been dating long-distance. And as I settled in at ESPN, MSG offered me a chance to come to games and live broadcasts. They had the Yankees, the Mets, all the winter sports -- Devils, Rangers, Islanders, Knicks and Liberty. So I started there in 1995, mostly doing baseball, the Yankees and Mets. Then after about 10 years, the Yankees and Mets each formed their own networks.

"So, then the Executive Producer at the time, came to me and said, 'How would you like to host the Islanders?' And I said, 'I'm in.' I jumped at the chance. So I did the Islanders for 10 years and then Doc Emrick was leaving the Devils to pursue national full-time. He was not going to be able to do both as he had for so many years. So, as sorry as we were to lose Doc, Steve Cangialosi got bumped upstairs to be the main play-by-play and Lou Lamoriello asked The Garden to trade me. So I got traded from the Islanders to the Devils.

"I didn't leave MSG, I just traded teams. It was a huge compliment at the time, although I remember being very sad to leave the Islanders. They were a great bunch of guys. John Tarvares had just finished his rookie year. Josh Bailey had been there a couple of years and they were a young, exciting team on the rise. I really enjoyed my time with the Islanders, but it was onto a new chapter and a new chance to cover a team and travel and go to every game, all 82 games a year. So that's what happened and I did the Devils for seven years."

MOST UNFORGETTABLE DEVILS GAME

If you ask any Devils fan who they feel is New Jersey's biggest rival, the answer you'll get every time is, the New York Rangers. And with good reason. Both teams play in the same division. Both teams play within close proximity of each other. And, going back throughout history, New Jersey has always had a rivalry of sorts with New York and not just in sports. In fact, the late, great owner of the Devils, Dr. John McMullen, always insisted that the Rangers never be mentioned on his team's radio broadcasts.

So it's understandable that these two teams have a certain amount of disdain for each other and that disdain has only intensified over the years. Of course, on the rare occasions that they meet in the playoffs, that disdain and intensity ratchets up another notch or two, or a hundred.

By my count, the Devils have faced the Rangers six times in the playoffs, with their most recent encounter taking place during the 2012 Eastern Conference Final.

Of course, their meeting in 2012 drew many comparisons to their epic battle in the 1994 Eastern Conference Final, which the Rangers won on a double-overtime goal in Game 7. And just like in 1994, there was a feeling in 2012 that the Rangers and Devils were on a collision course. So, when both secured their spots in the Eastern Conference Final, you just knew there was something special in the air, although neither side will likely ever admit to that.

Could New Jersey avenge its 1994 loss in 2012?

Well, the series started out pretty similar. The Devils and Rangers split the first two games at The Garden before New York captured Game 3 in New Jersey to take a 2-1 lead in the series.

Then, the Devils held the Rangers to a single goal in Game 4 to tie the series before winning Game 5 at Madison Square Garden to set up a potential elimination game in Game 6 back in New Jersey.

Boy, talk about Déjà vu!

Oh, and in case you needed any more similarities, Game 6 in both 1994 and 2012 was played on May 25th.

But there was one major difference. In 1994, Rangers' captain Mark Messier "guaranteed" a Game 6 victory and then pulled off a third period natural hat-trick to seal the deal. In 2012, Rangers' captain Ryan Callahan made no such bold declaration, nor did he have the type of game Messier did. Although he did manage to have one big moment. But I'll get to that in a minute.

DEB PLACEY: "The big games were always bigger for us too as broadcasters. We felt it. We wanted it to be that way. We did more. We were so prepared. I mean, we were always prepared for every game during the regular season, but in the playoffs it just felt bigger. After getting all the interviews for that night and doing all the work at the morning skate -- watching, writing, interviewing -- I had lunch with Steve Cangialosi. That's what we always did. He was my lunch partner. And then we would go back to the arena and get to our work. I would start writing my show, picking the sound bites, go into the truck and decide which sound bites fit where. We'd then fit them into the pre-game. And then, pretty soon, it would be time for the production meeting at four o'clock."

And pretty soon, once the production meeting was over, it was game time!

And just like they did in 1994, the Devils jumped out to an early 2-0 lead in the first period. But instead of the goals being scored by Scott

Niedermayer and Claude Lemieux, Ryan Carter and Ilya Kovalchuk scored them. (Kovalchuk's was a power-play goal).

From there the intensity grew, as fans of both teams could not believe what they were seeing.

The Devils carried that 2-0 lead into the second period, but goaltender Martin Brodeur had a bit of a brief flashback and a rather unpleasant one at that as the Rangers came back to tie the game at 2, courtesy of goals by Ruslan Fedotenko and, of course, Rangers' captain Ryan Callahan.

Mark Messier and Ryan Callahan, two Rangers captains, 18 years apart, managed to score the tying-goal against Martin Brodeur in Game 6 of the Eastern Conference Final. And both times the game was played in New Jersey.

But, luckily for the Devils, that's where the similarities between the two series finally ended.

A scoreless third period gave way to overtime, but it was brief.

DEB PLACEY: "I remember that, prior to the Rangers-Devils Game 6, back in the first round, the Devils didn't know until late who their opponent was going to be. But that had more to do with how Florida finished than them. They were locked into their spot. And as it turned out, they ended up facing the Panthers, in what was actually a long series.

"And I remember being down on the ice at the morning skate and saying to someone how Adam Henrique had had a wonderful rookie season and how he had tailed off a little bit at the end, but that he was going to be nominated for the Calder.

"He had made enough of a name for himself and there wasn't a Connor McDavid or a Sidney Crosby type rookie who had 100 points. So he was in the mix for sure. But he hadn't done much in that first round series. And I remember saying, 'I'd like to see Adam do something tonight.'

"And then, of course, he went on and scored the double-overtime game-winner. So, to fast forward to Game 6 against the Rangers, there was a chance for this to be an elimination game, for the Rangers. And it was also a chance for the Devils to advance to the Stanley Cup Final.

"Now, Adam had gotten a reputation during the regular season as a clutch player, because he always seemed to score big goals. But he also seemed to make big plays in important moments. He'd be on the ice in any situation. He could play on the penalty-kill. He was a great defensive forward. Even as a rookie, he was relied upon by Pete DeBoer and the coaching staff to be on the ice in every situation. And this is such a simple statement, but he never did anything dumb with the puck.

"And so, getting back to the game, in overtime, I remember it was quick. Henrik Lundqvist was on the ground having managed to keep the puck out of the net during a scramble. And then Adam, who was positioned next to Lundqvist, scored and then immediately turned his head to the right and headed for the glass, jumping up and down.

"Now, that so happened to be the corner where we stood to watch the games every night during the regular season. That was the broadcast position where we would also do our live hits from, on camera. "And that's where I would've been if it wasn't overtime. But we had to be in the studio sitting on the set because the game could end at any time.

"So he ran and jumped onto the glass. But I saw it like everybody else did, from far up in the stands where our set was. I wasn't right there where we normally would be, which is kind of funny. He was just such a wonderful young man. And it was a tough thing when he got traded during the 2017-18 season. We got to know his family while he was here in Jersey. He grew up on a tobacco farm and basically said, 'I don't want to be a tobacco farmer.' So that kept him working hard. Adam was always working hard. Always the first one in the gym in the morning and the first one on the ice. And he was always the last to leave.

"So that game is my favorite because of how exciting it was because of the high stakes and also because Henrique was one of my favorite people on the planet.

"And after Henrique scored, that was the fastest I'd ever seen Marty Brodeur move. Marty came down the ice to the other end to come celebrate. He loved beating Henrik Lundqvist. Lundqvist had gotten the better of Marty in the regular season. And then, of course, Mike Richter was in goal when the Rangers beat Broduer and the Devils to go to the Stanley Cup in 1994, which was Marty's rookie season. But Marty finally got the best of them. And I also remember Ryan McDonagh, just unable to move as the Devils were jumping up and down celebrating. Both teams were absolutely spent, but it's such a different feeling when you win."

MOST UNFORGETTABLE DEVILS MOMENT

PLACEY: "My favorite (moment) would be Marty Brodeur's retirement. His number 30 going up to the rafters. I have a picture of Marty coming over to sit with us and him and I on the set just sharing a laugh and having him talk about what it meant to him to see his number go up and to be there with his family. Missing his dad, who would have loved that moment and got him started playing and just everything leading up to it. How much Marty meant to all of his teammates. To see him share that weekend with all of his teammates and with all of the fans and with the staff and his old coaches and everything. To have them be so candid and talk about it and get a little emotional. To be with him at that is probably my favorite Devils' memory."

14 GLENN "CHICO RESCH (NJ DEVILS)
FIRST WIN IN TEAM HISTORY (@BRENDAN BYRNE ARENA)
OCTOBER 8, 1982
NJD 3, NYR 2

BACKGROUND

When it comes to the man known as Glenn "Chico" Resch, or just "Chico" as he is normally referred to, chances are you won't find a more jovial person throughout the entire National Hockey League. As one of the All-Time greatest characters, both on and off the ice, Chico is just as likely to wow you with a story from his playing days as he is to knock your socks off with a terrific bit of comedic timing. Of course, it's also a good idea to have a stopwatch or something handy, because when you enter a conversation with Chico, you're likely to be in it for quite awhile.

Glenn Resch was born in Moose Jaw, Saskatchewan, and from an early age, professional hockey was in his sights.

"I went through all the channels," as Resch likes to put it. "I played kid's hockey and then a little bit of Junior and then I played in College before going to Montreal Training Camp. Then I got traded to the Islanders the year after they entered the league. I played there for a bit, (and won the Stanley Cup in 1979-80), before getting traded to Colorado. And when the Rockies were sold and moved to New Jersey I went with them before eventually finishing my playing career in Philadelphia.

"After that, I coached in Junior for a little while," continued Resch. "Then I was the Assistant Coach and Goalie Coach in Ottawa. Eventually, I got the offer to do television with New Jersey and I accepted that. I did that for 18 years with Doc Emrick before retiring for

112

two years. And now I'm back doing radio with Matt Loughlin and the New Jersey Devils again."

(For those of you wondering how a man of so many words seemingly didn't have much to say about his playing career, I should admit, I indeed had a stopwatch handy.)

MOST UNFORGETTABLE DEVILS GAMES

The first of anything in the history of a franchise is always important -- and memorable. And when that franchise first comes against your primary rival, it's made all the sweeter.

So, when the newly rebranded Devils began play in their new digs in the fall of 1982, there were some questions that needed answering.

One, how good would this team be? Two, would the fans embrace this team as their own? Three, could this team compete with its "Big Brother" type of rival, the New York Rangers? And four, when would this team get its first win?

As it turned out, questions two, three and four would be answered at the same time.

Having ended the opening game of their season against Pittsburgh in a tie, the Devils and their small, yet growing following, were still in search of their first win since moving to the Garden State when lo and behold, the Rangers came to town.

These two teams hadn't yet faced off against each other and there was already animosity between them.

First, the Devils had to pay the Rangers for the right to move to New Jersey. (They also had to pay the Islanders and Flyers, with the combined compensation to the three teams approximating $20 million).

Secondly, the Devils' owner, Dr. John McMullen, wanted his team to be unique and to embrace the fact they were New Jersey's team. (The NFL's Jets and Giants certainly didn't). Dr. McMullen even ordered his team's radio play-by-play man Larry Hirsch, to not mention anything about the Rangers on his broadcasts.

So, with these two teams about to face-off for the first time, it was clear that this wouldn't be just any game. And who was the starting goaltender for New Jersey? It was Chico Resch.

CHICO RESCH: "Our first year, second game, we were at home and we played the New York Rangers. Herb Brooks was coaching the Rangers and I think the score was 3-2."

And a big reason why the Devils won that game was that Resch made 21 of 23 saves to stifle the Rangers. And while Resch was keeping the puck out of the Devils' net, New Jersey was putting pucks past Blueshirts' netminder, John Davidson.

A first period power-play goal from Steve Tambellini opened the scoring. And even though New York tied it early in the second period on a goal from Anders Hedberg, it never felt like New Jersey was losing its momentum. And Bob MacMillan proved that when he scored the go-ahead goal almost nine minutes later.

Of course, the Rangers didn't want to go quietly as Mark Pavelich tied the game 19 seconds later.

But one final goal for New Jersey, this one a power-play marker from Merlin Malinowski late in the second period, managed to put New York away and set off a celebration in New Jersey.

CHICO RESCH: "That moment was as special as any that I had with the Devils, because we beat our rivals, the Rangers. I think it helped solidify the fan base we had. We were just starting, so we didn't have a huge wide fan base. But I think it got them excited and solidified that. And then, I just remember celebrating with the players after and what a good feeling it was. I mean, that didn't last long. That was a tough year. But I've got to tell you, winning that first game against the Rangers in the Meadowlands, was as satisfying as any game I had as a New Jersey Devil.

"The great thing about playing the Rangers was it didn't take any special preparation. You just automatically, the switches were turned on. And, even though, I remember the fan base was probably 50-50 cheering for us. It was still our home game. It was still a moment that I think the players recognized as, if we wanted to get some respect early on, this was a good game to win. And I mean the Rangers game, you hear this all the time so it's only cliché, but you just don't have to get fired up for him. You just walk in and you know it's a Rangers game and there's a little extra buzz in the air with the fans. It was a good, close game, so it wasn't like it was lucky. It was a well-earned victory and it was very, very satisfying.

"I remember, when the horn went off and the excitement and satisfaction we all had individually, but then, as we celebrated on the ice, it was the moment that athletes, hockey players play for, where you have this huge challenge. And not only did we overcome it, but we also didn't succumb to the pressure. I mean there are exciting moments, but it's more, the satisfying feeling that athletes get when they don't cave in. We were confronted and we were challenged and we stood up to it all and we didn't break down. The moment that big horn went off in the Meadowlands, we knew we had won our first game against our rival."

And just like that, the Devils had their first win in team history.

MOST UNFORGETTABLE DEVILS MOMENTS

CHICO RESCH: ""Well, you know, that's a tough question, because as an athlete, there's so many. I think I would go back to Marty (Brodeur) scoring the goal (in the 1997 playoffs against Montreal) and how high he jumped to celebrate it. That's kind of etched in my very being having been a goalie and now as an announcer and to see Marty score the goal, which, for a goalie, is really unheard of. And to see how he jumped, I'll never forget that moment.

"And then (for a moment from my playing career), I remember, we'd never beaten the Islanders and we were ahead of them (this was when I was a goalie for New Jersey) and we were winning 2-0. I don't know which referee it was, but the Islanders were starting to complain. I had a shutout going and we were playing really well. And the Islanders were just screaming at the officials about penalties. I said to one of the referees, 'those guys were just crying over there. They're just frustrated. We've never beaten them and I'm just encouraging you, don't let them affect you. Don't call a cheap penalty.'

"Well, maybe that made him mad, because right at the end of that period, I was standing in my crease, looking in the corner and one of the Isles players comes by, skates through crease, hits my stick and dives. I didn't even see him coming. I did not trip him. I looked at the referee and he's got his hand up. I'm thinking, 'he can't be calling a penalty on me?' Sure enough, he calls the tripping penalty and I lost it. I threw my glove way up in the air. I mean it wasn't a good move. I threw my glove. I dropped my stick.

"And I've seen a picture of that moment, because the ironic thing was, I got that penalty and they scored right at the end of the period. And then they scored early in the third on the power-play. Of course, then Mike Bossy won it in overtime and we didn't beat them. We beat them later on, but we didn't win that game. But I think me flipping out like that, it was a temper tantrum at its finest. And that glove flying up in the air, it went way up. And I could see why he had to call an extra two minutes. But my goodness, it was a bad call."

15 CHRIS RYAN (NJ ADVANCE MEDIA)
"MVP! MVP! MVP!" (@PRUDENTIAL CENTER)
APRIL 3, 2018
NJD 5, NYR 2

BACKGROUND

Every so often it's important to have an influx of new blood, regardless of what industry you're in. And the media who cover the New Jersey Devils is no different.

So, as we move into a new Era of Devils hockey and a new generation of Devils fans comes of age, it's essential that they have a group of writers who they can connect with and grow with as the years go on. And in New Jersey, it just so happens that that influx of new talent is happening as we speak. Writers such as: Corey Masisak, Leo Scaglione Jr., myself and, of course, Chris Ryan, are tasked with continuing to uphold the proud traditions of Devils' coverage as the new generation blossoms.

For Chris Ryan, the opportunity to cover his hometown team is, to paraphrase The Godfather, "an offer he couldn't refuse."

So, I'm just going to "leave the gun and take the cannoli" as Chris tells you his story.

CHRIS RYAN: "I grew up in Monroe, in Middlesex County. I grew up around the Devils. I honestly wasn't a big hockey fan. I wasn't a big Devils fan growing up, but I, of course, knew the team. I knew the history. I knew the franchise. When you grow up around a team that wins three Stanley Cups, you're going to know a lot about them.

"And I think, like with any sports writer, you grow up with a passion for sports and that kind of translated into a journalism career. When I was in college, I actually started off as a biology major for two years. I did that, didn't really like it. So I kind of took a chance and went into journalism. And then, I ended up working at the college paper, up there at *The Daily Collegian at Penn State* and loved it immediately.

"So that kind of started my sports journalism career. I did that for a year-and-a-half there and then, when I graduated from college in the summer of 2012, I started looking for jobs. As many people know it's kind of tough. You're looking for anywhere to get your foot in the door and luckily for me, *The Star-Ledger* had an opening for a part-time, high school sports reporter. So, I took a two-day a week job covering boys soccer in Morris County for the Fall of 2012.

"I started doing that and then, that kind of led to a full-time position the following year. I did high school sports for four years total with *The Ledger*. And when Rich Chere left in the spring of 2016, my boss approached me about taking over the Devils beat and I jumped on it. And I just finished my third season covering the Devils. It's certainly been a dream to cover a pro-team. I mean, I don't think I could have asked for a better starting point in terms of a team to cover and just what kind of history this franchise has and what I've been able to do so far."

MOST UNFORGETTABLE DEVILS GAME

The 2017-18 Devils were a surprise, plain and simple. After missing the playoffs every year since losing to the Los Angeles Kings in the 2012 Stanley Cup Final, there was no reason to believe that New Jersey was on the verge of a turnaround. However, the best surprises are those we don't see coming.

After a last place finish in the Metropolitan Division in the 2016-17 season, the Devils received their first surprise, though this one wasn't so unexpected. They received the right to draft first overall at the NHL's Annual Entry Draft in June 2017. And with that pick, they had a difficult choice.

There were two highly regarded prospects as the top of the draft class. One was Nolan Patrick and the other was Nico Hischier. And many analysts favored Patrick over Hischier. But in typical Ray Shero fashion, the General Manager of the Devils refused to disclose his preference until he was standing on the stage at the draft, with New Jersey on the clock. And it was at that moment that Shero made a move that helped set the stage for a surprising Devils season, for he selected Nico Hischier with the Number One overall selection.

Of course, his counterpart in Philadelphia -- the Flyers held the second pick -- Ron Hextall, was equally ecstatic, as the move meant he could get his guy, Nolan Patrick. And while many felt Patrick would indeed have the better rookie season, that didn't sway Shero's thought process one bit. And it certainly didn't sway Head Coach, John Hynes' thoughts either, as Hynes was over the moon about having Hischier in the fold.

And when the Devils won nine of their first 11 games, all was right in New Jersey. Hischier was coming along at a brisk pace, with seven points in his first seven games. And Taylor Hall was showing signs that this was going to be HIS YEAR, with nine points in those seven contests.

But while the Devils eventually came back down to Earth and Hischier had a slightly inconsistent, yet still superb rookie year, Hall proved that he was not going to be stopped by anyone.

From January 2, 2018, through March 6, 2018, a span of 26 games, Hall registered an astounding 18 goals and 20 assists -- 38 points -- all while fueling the engine that was the Devils' attempt to get back to the playoffs. And, during those 26 games, Hall never went without a point. So it was no wonder when fans started to chant, "MVP!" whenever he touched the puck.

Meanwhile, New Jersey needed every last point it could get as a mid-season swoon threatened to undo Hall's brilliance. But fear not, for Hall kicked things into overdrive. And when the hated Rangers came to town on April 3, 2018, there was a sense that this could be a make or break game for the Devils.

New Jersey was on the cusp of clinching a playoff berth, but a loss could just as easily have prevented them from doing so. And even though the Rangers were in the midst of missing the playoffs for the first time since the 2009-10 season, nobody needed to tell either side just how important this game was going to be.

And Taylor Hall was up to the challenge.

CHRIS RYAN: "They were certainly in a good head space heading into that game. They had rattled off such a good run in March to get to that point. And the Panthers had just done the same thing. So they needed every one of those wins. But, every test they faced, they came out of it in good shape.

"And you kind of got the vibe that, 'hey, this team knows what it takes to win and get in.' They understood the ramifications and they knew they couldn't get too high against the Rangers because they were in the same spot a year ago when one of their final games was against the Rangers, who were in a similar spot of needing wins to get in.

"So, it was the third to final game of the season. They were still fighting off the Panthers, trying to hold on for that last playoff spot. And they essentially needed to win, probably two of their final three games to get in. So they're hosting the Rangers. It's a big rivalry and the Rangers were out of, but it didn't matter. You were going to get the best of them every night. And, at the same time, Taylor Hall was going through his MVP run and he went off for four points that night and the Devils wound up winning that game. And it kind of helped to solidify his MVP status by helping them get within a win of the playoffs.

"It's a game they needed to win and they came out, Travis Zajac scored a goal in the first minute or two. Taylor Hall added a goal later in that first period. So, they had an early lead and they were not messing around."

No, the Devils definitely weren't messing around. Rookie Will Butcher even chipped in two power-play goals of his own to help boost New Jersey's lead to 4-1 -- the Rangers got on the board with a goal from Ryan Spooner. But Taylor Hall was about to drop the hammer on their cross-river rivals.

CHRIS RYAN: "The thing that capped it off was Taylor Hall's penalty shot later in the second period. They were up 4-1 at the time and he already had three points. I mean, everyone in the arena stood and you just kind of got the sense that the shot was going to go in.

"There was no way this guy was missing the shot. He stepped up -- Taylor Hall is a finesse guy, he can use his hands around the net -- and he just wound up for a slap shot, middle of the dots, drilled the puck past Henrik Lundqvist and the arena went nuts."

The Devils fans in attendance were raining down "MVP!" chants on Hall as his shot whizzed past Lundqvist. It was so deafening that the reporters covering the game couldn't hear themselves think. But most importantly, the goal was the final nail in the coffin, as it was New Jersey's fifth and final goal of the game.

CHRIS RYAN: "The goal gave the Devils a 5-1 lead, which they easily held onto for the eventual 5-2 win. And that set-up a game against the Maple Leafs two days later to clinch a playoff spot. But that was kind of just the cherry on top of that season. That game, they weren't messing around, they needed to win and they did everything they could and just dominated their rival, who could have easily have beaten them on any given night."

MOST UNFORGETTABLE DEVILS MOMENT

CHRIS RYAN: "I'm gonna go with Opening Night of the 2017-18 season, because they were coming off that year where they finished in last place in The East, but they ended up getting the Number One pick, which they used to get Nico Hischier. It felt, to me, kind of like that turning point for this team. It's Year Three of Ray Shero and John Hynes and certainly they had a good first year, but that second year, when you bottom out and finish in last place, it left the franchise and the fans with a lot of questions. And that off-season sort of set the tone (for the 2017-18 season). I can remember that pre-game, when Nico was introduced, the fans went nuts. They had the opening video montage and Nico was the lead of that. And it just kind of set the tone.

"Also, Brian Boyle was going through his cancer treatment at that point. He got introduced from the bench and he got the loudest ovation, bigger than Nico's. For how well they started the year and what they did all year, it was just a special night that kind of set the tone and oddly enough, it kind of reflected what they eventually went through."

16 BRYCE SALVADOR (NJ DEVILS)
SAY GOOD-BYE TO 1994! HENRIQUE SLAYS THE RANGERS!
(@PRUDENTIAL CENTER)
MAY 25, 2012
NJD 3, NYR 2 (OT)

BACKGROUND

When Zach Parise left New Jersey for a chance to go home to Minnesota, many Devils fans questioned who would fill the leadership void on the team.

Well, they didn't have to wait long for an answer as New Jersey named Bryce Salvador as its new captain. And Salvador was born for the job.

With the type of personality and skill set that Salvador had, he was a natural fit for the captaincy. And while the Devils did not make the playoffs during his three-season tenure with the "C," he did everything in his power to help nurture the next generation of Devils players; and we are now beginning to see the fruits of his labor.

But how did the Brandon, Manitoba native end up with the Devils?

BRYCE SALVADOR: "Well, I think I played hockey because I was a Canadian boy growing up in a culture where that's all we did. Everyone in my class, everyone in my neighborhood, we all had skates. We had outdoor rinks in our area. I grew up in Brandon, Manitoba. So, it was just one of those activities that everyone did. Just the fact that we had outdoor rinks and you could skate as much as you wanted to; there was no structure, everyone just let you go and have fun. Especially in the '70s, '80s and '90s, a lot of Canadian hockey players were produced.

Some great players came through those generations. It was cool to play hockey and that's why I played."

There certainly were a lot of great hockey players who hailed from Canada during that time period. After all, hockey IS Canada's game. And that tradition of breeding tremendous hockey players is still alive to this day.

For Bryce Salvador, that was just the first step on his path to becoming one of the most respected players and now broadcasters, in the game.

BRYCE SALVADOR: "I didn't necessarily know the path to make it to the NHL. I turned the TV on and the Oilers were winning another Stanley Cup. And it just seemed like something out of reach. For my family, and me, we had no hockey players in our background. And it was just something I enjoyed. For whatever reason, I continued to improve and develop and then teams started to take notice of me. The first team was the Lethbridge Hurricanes in the WHL. They happened to be watching the Brandon Wheat Kings of the WHL and my Bantam team happened to be playing before that WHL game.

"As the story goes, they were scouting my D-partner, because they thought for sure the Brandon Wheat Kings would have had me protected. But that wasn't the case. So when they went back, they said, 'Geez, we're going to protect this Salvador kid and bring him to camp.' So I went to camp at 16-years-old.

"I always like to tell the story that I had a toothbrush and a pair of jeans and the next thing I know they were like, 'you're staying.' My dad and I were like, 'what do you mean we're staying?' And they said, 'Well, you're going to stay here and live here and play.'

"We were like, 'Okay, but I better ask my mom first if it's okay.' That just spoke to the volume of how naive we were with the process of making it to the NHL. That first step, for us, was the WHL. And when it happened, I spent five years with the Lethbridge Hurricanes and then I was drafted by Tampa Bay.

"Things didn't work out with Tampa Bay. It was my first adversity in a professional environment, in the WHL. Having an Expansion team say, 'Kid, you're not good, go to school. Beyond the WHL is probably not your path.' Learning from that and being able to grow from it was very important.

"Fast forward to my last year in the WHL, I was 20-years-old and it was my overage year. I came in with the right mindset and had a phenomenal season. Before I knew it, I signed with the St. Louis Blues as a free agent and we went to the Memorial Cup, where we lost in The Finals. The next couple of months, I was in Worcester, Massachusetts,

122

playing for the Worcester IceCats in the AHL. St. Louis was sharing an AHL franchise with the San Jose Sharks.

"I spent three years there and that was the next little journey for myself in developing and understanding the game and learning and realizing that this was a business and what I needed to do to be a professional. I put my time in there and then my career started with the St. Louis Blues. My first game was against the Phoenix Coyotes, I looked across and there was future Hall-of-Famer, Al MacInnis as my D-partner.

"I was like, 'Wow, I've sure come a long way from Brandon, Manitoba, skating at an outdoor rink.'

"I spent seven years with St. Louis and then I was traded when my contract came up. It was going to be the first time I was a free agent and the Devils liked the way I played. It was one of those where I don't know if I would have signed there as a free agent. I didn't know anything about New Jersey. I didn't know anything about the Eastern Conference. Most likely, I would have stayed in the Western Conference. But because of that trade and seeing what the culture was like under Lou Lamoriello, it just really resonated with me. It really meshed with the style of game that I played.

"Lou allowed me to play to my identity and it just afforded me an opportunity to continue my career and continue to build a relationship with the fans, the organization and the community. After the 2012 Cup run Zach Parise left and there was a void, which worked out because of the point where I was at in my career and being named the captain was something I was ready for."

After being named Captain for the start of the 2012-13 season, Salvador served in that capacity until he retired following the conclusion of the 2014-15 campaign.

And while he was enjoying his retirement from playing, Salvador did stay involved with hockey by coaching at the grassroots level and running a pro-shop. But little did he know, the NHL was preparing to pull him back in; not as a player, but as a broadcaster. MSG Network was experiencing a bit of a turnover in terms of on-air personalities and a social media post was making the rounds speculating about if Salvador would be the one to replace the departing John MacLean.

In fact, Salvador himself didn't know about it until his wife mentioned it to him. So he reached out to MSG Networks and spoke to Katie Epifane about the opening, but in a rather casual way. And the next day, when he spoke to the Devils, it was mentioned to him that his name had come up in the conversations regarding the position. From there he went through several interviews and "tests" before landing the gig. And while he was, by his own admission, "learning on the job," it is a role that he has filled valiantly since the 2017-18 season and one that he will hopefully continue to hold for years to come.

MOST UNFORGETTABLE DEVILS GAME

While Bryce Salvador has endeared himself to Devils fans as both a player and broadcaster, it was during his playing days that he experienced his "Most Unforgettable Devils" game. And boy was it a memorable one!

The year before Salvador became captain (2011-12), the Devils were one of the best teams in the league and that was due, in no small part, to the brilliance of their new Head Coach, Pete DeBoer. Under DeBoer, the Devils jelled perfectly and accumulated 102 points during the regular season.

And come playoff time, New Jersey was a force to be reckoned with. With triumphs over the Panthers and Flyers complete, the Devils moved onto the Eastern Conference Final where they went toe to toe with their archrivals, the New York Rangers.

With only four wins standing between the Devils and a trip to the Stanley Cup Final, the Garden Staters knew they had to take care of business against the Rangers. And even though the series played out in eerily similar fashion to the epic Eastern Conference Final these teams contested in 1994, this was also an opportunity for New Jersey to get some long awaited revenge.

So, with the Devils leading the series 3-2 going into Game 6 at the Prudential Center, New Jersey finally had its chance to knock off New York and put to bed the memory of 1994.

BRYCE SALVADOR: "I was a very structured guy. It was just one of those things where it was a lot of mental preparation. What I was doing during that Stanley Cup playoff series and really the whole playoffs, was just visualizing the game in the mornings and visualizing how certain plays might happen in certain situations. If there's a possibility for an odd-man rush, I want to visualize when to jump into the play. I wanted to visualize how the Rangers were probably going to be fore-checking.

"Everyone knew the importance of Game 6. Everyone was ready for that game. You understood the importance of the game. I liked to keep the guys loose and joke a little bit. But we had a special team and I knew that if we just stuck to our game plan that we were going to get through to the next round. There really was nothing to be tweaked. We were playing great hockey

"I think the way that series was going, I don't think anyone on our roster wanted to go back to Madison Square Garden for Game 7; that's for sure. The momentum was in our favor, especially in Game 6.

"We went up two goals. I believe it was 2-0 and then the Rangers started coming back. They tied it up and you could just feel the needles and the pin drops in that arena, because you had a lot of Rangers fans there too. Obviously, I wasn't in the '94 series, but just the atmosphere, to have that many fans who are rooting against you in your own building, kind of clashing. There was almost a separate game being played within the fans, especially when we scored."

The Devils certainly were pushing the pace of the game in the first period and their goals from Ryan Carter and Ilya Kovalchuk were proof of that. But the ice began to get tilted in the second period as the Rangers found some extra energy. And when Ruslan Fedotenko and Ryan Callahan scored to tie the game, things became a bit tense at Prudential Center.

BRYCE SALVADOR: "When they tied it up, my feeling was like, 'Whoa, we've got a game here.' You had to give them a lot of credit for coming back and not rolling over. And you also had to realize, if the Rangers win the game, then they're building momentum and heading home for Game 7. But we had the mindset of, 'this was our turn now.'

"When we got up ahead and then the Rangers caught up, the way the crowd just started rooting for the Rangers, it was just that atmosphere really. I remember how exciting it was and then when it went to overtime, I started feeling like, 'we've got this.' You could just feel the way that the zonetime, the pressure, we were going. Kolvy (Ilya Kovalchuk) was having one of those games and sure enough, he was a big factor on the overtime goal.

"I remember, Kovalchuk was on the ice and there was a scrum in front of the net. From my vantage point, Kovalchuk was attacking and Henrique was off to the side and then, obviously, for Henry (Adam Henrique) to bury that rebound there and to bank it in. He was young but he was like a wily veteran on that goal. His celebration and the famous photograph of him going to the glass, that kind of fortifies the memory for me. Just the whole playoffs that year for the Devils, being a part of that myself, it was surreal.

"And I remember, after the goal was scored, Ryan McDonagh was on his knees, just kind of looking out and realizing that it was over.

"It's a great memory for me that we beat the Rangers to go to the Stanley Cup Final."

MOST UNFORGETTABLE DEVILS MOMENT

SALVADOR: "(As a player, my favorite moment would be) the game-winning goal in Game Five (of the 2012 Stanley Cup Final against the Kings). My hands were up in the air. I scored the second goal. It was kind of fluky; the puck definitely had eyes. But just the celebration after that. We were just starting to mount a comeback. We were in a huge hole in that series and that game gave us more life. Honestly, I would say that I think that whole year would be my favorite memory. I had just come back. I missed a whole year from a concussion, and then, not even a year later I was scoring a game-winning goal in the Stanley Cup Final. I think that'd be a good snapshot from my (playing) career.

"(And as a broadcaster, my favorite moment would be) when Andreas Athanasiou came into my box. We actually have a photo of it. Basically, it was a penalty. There were too many men on the ice and the puck came over to the bench and he was like, 'I've got to get off the ice,' and 'hey, I'm going to go pay Salvador a visit.' It was interesting, because it was almost like a matrix scene.

"I felt like it was in slow motion of him coming over the bench and I'm like, 'Is he going to land on my feet and cut my toes off? Do I have to get my elbow up and knock him back over? Can I hit him or not hit him? Is that crossing the line? Do I push him? What happens if I hit him and he falls back over and gets injured?' All in a matter of a split second, all of those things were going through my mind and luckily I just was able to kind of take a step back and I was ready to react if I had to. But he didn't land on me. He looked over and realized he was not supposed to be in there and he jumped back out and the refs missed it."

17 LEO SCAGLIONE JR. (NY HOCKEY JOURNAL & THE FISCHLER REPORT) DEVILS CLINCH 1ST PLAYOFF BERTH SINCE 2012 (@PRUDENTIAL CENTER) APRIL 5, 2018 NJD 2, TOR 1

BACKGROUND

To most, the world of professional sports must seem very vast. And that doubles for the world of the sports media too. But in actuality, both worlds are rather small and exist on the same plane.

So therefore, it's noteworthy when a new, young writer joins the ranks. Usually, that writer has paid his or her dues through a variety of internships or by simply persevering through whatever means necessary. And one of the best young writers to join the ranks of the media, who cover the New Jersey Devils, is Leo Scaglione Jr.

Scaglione Jr. boasts an impressive set of bylines that include, but are not limited to: *The Fischler Report*, The *NY Hockey Journal* and *The Hockey Writers*. And from the time he started writing about hockey, at various levels, through to his present day gig covering the Devils, Scaglione Jr. has become a must-read source of information for New Jersey's fan base.

But how did he accomplish something that so many want and so few get?

LEO SCAGLIONE JR.: "As a kid, my parents were New York Rangers fans, so I fell in love with the sport at a very early age. The big moment came in 1995, the first round, the eight-seeded Rangers upset the Number One Quebec Nordiques and so my family was excited about that. However, in the second round the Flyers swept the Rangers. And at that point, I wanted to see more hockey. I wasn't content with the season being over. So my parents put on the next round, which was the Eastern Conference Final and it was the Flyers against the Devils.

"I cheered for the Devils because the Flyers beat my family's Rangers. And the thing was my favorite color, as a kid, was red and the Devils had this goaltender with a really cool name.

"So that solidified my love for the sport. And then, of course, I ended up following this particular team, for almost ever it feels like. But as a kid, when I was watching the Devils, I'd always put the game as a whole, whether it was the NHL, the minor leagues, international hockey, whatever it may be, on the same level. I just enjoyed the game as a whole and followed it religiously. At the same time, as a kid, I loved reading and writing. And I remember, I was called a bookworm as a kid too, because I was always holding a book in my hand while everyone else was outside during the summer playing.

"So it really became, as I got older, a matter of how do I put this together? My love for reading, for writing and my love for hockey. And I was fortunate that I met Dan Rice around 2012, 2013 and he wrote for *The Hockey Writers* covering the Devils.

"And in 2013, *The Hockey Writers* were looking to expand their coverage into the American Hockey League. And I was familiar with because of the Albany Devils because of their connection with New Jersey. So I said, 'you know what, I'll take this challenge. Let's do it.' So I started covering the Albany Devils for *The Hockey Writers*. After half a season, they didn't want to cover the American League as much anymore. So, some of the American League writers ended up covering the NHL teams.

"I stayed on covering the Devils for the rest of that season and then in the fall of 2014, I started interning for Stan Fischler and writing for the *Fischler Report*.

"And I added The *New York Hockey Journal* to my arsenal in the spring of 2015, on the Devils beat and one year later, at the 2016 Draft, I added the Islanders beat. Since then, I have covered the game at all different levels, whether it's the NHL, American League, College, Juniors and Prospects. That's where I'm at today."

MOST UNFORGETTABLE DEVILS GAME

When the 2017-18 season got underway, the New Jersey Devils were hoping for a turnaround. But nobody had any idea what was in store for the club.

With the talented, yet inexperienced rookie, Nico Hischier in the fold and Taylor Hall having an MVP-season, the Devils ended up being a surprise playoff contestant. But that doesn't mean they had it easy getting to the playoffs, because the grueling grind of the regular season was anything but easy.

And even though Hall had a superlative year, the Garden Staters still scuffled at times. But in the end, everything balanced out as the team entered the final week of the season eyeing its first playoff berth since the spring of 2012.

However, just because they were eyeing a playoff berth, that doesn't mean that the other teams in the Eastern Conference just rolled over and let the Devils, have their way. And that was especially true of the Florida Panthers, who battled New Jersey in the standings down to the penultimate day of the season.

Following a win at home against their archrivals, the New York Rangers, the Devils controlled their own destiny. All they needed to do was beat the Toronto Maple Leafs in their second-to-last game of the season. If they could do that, they would clinch a spot in the Stanley Cup playoffs.

So, there the Devils were. They were on the doorstep of securing their first playoff berth in five seasons! That's an eternity in Devils Land.

It was April 5, 2018, and the Maple Leafs, who themselves were a playoff-bound team, were in town representing the last obstacle for this gritty New Jersey team. And who was there at Prudential Center to give his expert coverage? Just the man of the hour, or chapter, Leo Scaglione Jr.

LEO SCAGLIONE JR.: "It was their home finale and the Devils needed two points (to clinch a playoff berth). As long as they got the two points or the Florida Panthers didn't get two points they would clinch a playoff spot. And, of course, if you were at that game as a Devils fan, you were cheering for the Devils to win. From my perspective, all the way up at the top, (the press box is rather high up at Prudential Center), I wanted to see the Devils clinch a playoff spot because that'd be really cool (to cover).

"And I remember walking on the concourse at one point before the game, looking outside and the fans were lining up pretty early outside. There's a park that overlooks Championship Plaza right across from the Devils team store and the fans were there very early. So the excitement in and around the building was crazy. It was different. It had been just a couple of years already since they had been in the playoffs and just being able to possibly end that drought, it was exciting for the fans.

"Now, the thing is, entering this game, the Devils actually had an opportunity to clinch a couple of days earlier. They played the Rangers and beat the Rangers 5-2. The Devils came out, guns blazing that game. They scored in the opening minute on a goal from Travis Zajac. They added to their tally when Taylor Hall, who had an extremely memorable night from start to finish, scored on a penalty shot against Henrik Lundqvist. The Devils did their job that night. They got the two points. But the Panthers also won, so that meant the party in New Jersey would have to be delayed at least a couple of days.

"And now, the Devils had the ball (puck) in their own court against Toronto. They win and their in. The game started and the building was rocking and William Nylander scored early in the first period. It was kind of a fluky goal and it gave Toronto the 1-0 lead. And they took that lead into the first intermission.

"The second period started and the teams had plenty of back and forth action. And then Pavel Zacha, who got control of the puck at the left face-off dot, shot and scored. It's probably a goal that Freddy Andersen would want back, but Zacha scored to tie the game. And later on in that period, on one of the most horrible goals I've ever watched, Pat Maroon got the puck in the slot, went towards the far wall, carried the puck along the far wall between the face-off circle and the blue line, goes behind the net and from his spot, throws the puck towards the crease where Miles Wood was waiting for a one-timer and Wood does just that to give the Devils a 2-1 lead.

"Now, one thing about Maroon, he was one of the players that the Devils grabbed at the Trade Deadline. They had been buyers at the Trade Deadline for the first time in many years. So the fact that he was able to do what he just did was excellent. And I also remember, earlier in that period, Michael Grabner, who they also acquired at the deadline, had a breakaway that he almost scored on. So it was exciting in New Jersey, just from the background perspective because they were buyers and you were now seeing some of the players, who they bought, producing in a big game.

"So it was 2-1 New Jersey after that goal. The third period started back and forth and I remember the building having a combination of excitement and tension. It wasn't as tense as a playoff game and it wasn't a situation where they had to win, because they still had another game to play. Plus, the Panthers could still lose."

Not only could the Panthers still lose, but privately, many fans were probably hoping Florida would, for the Panthers had been hot and everybody knows that anything can happen on the final day of the season. It was important to get the win now, rather than to take any unnecessary chances.

LEO SCAGLIONE JR.: "The fans, at that point, they wanted to see their team win. The minutes were ticking down. Keith Kinkaid was in net. He had a tremendous second half that season and was one of the reasons the Devils ended up making the playoffs. He was making save after save and in the final moments, with roughly eight to 10 seconds left, the Leafs got a shot from the right point, it was a pretty good shot and Kinkaid smothered it. He kept it, forcing a face-off with like five seconds left in the game. The Devils won the face-off. They cleared the ice and that was it, they were in the playoffs for the first time since 2012.

"It was a special moment for the fan base because this was -- and is -- a fan base that was so used to winning for so long. Now they had gone through, what was for them, a drought. So to be able to get back to the playoffs for the first time in several years, it was special.

"And when the clock struck triple zero, I remember thinking that Lou Lamoriello was probably in the building, which means the Devils still to this day, the Devils team, not franchise, every time the team had made the playoffs, Lou Lamoriello was either in charge or at the very least, in the building. That was one of the first things I thought about when the clock hit zero.

"Meanwhile, after the game, I went to the Devils locker room and after every home finale, the players' families are usually in the room. So there were some family members around. And, of course, it was a very exciting room to be in at that moment.

"And one of the most memorable moments from that post-game, for me, came after the game. Brian Boyle was standing at his locker, being interviewed. And his son, Declan, walked over to him and Boyle picked him up. These were two people who had been through hell and back. Boyle had missed the beginning of the year with chronic myeloid leukemia. And Declan had been going through his own surgeries for an arteriovenous malformation in his jaw. And now, in that particular moment, Brian was holding Declan after having helped the Devils to reach the playoffs. It was pretty emotional."

MOST UNFORGETTABLE DEVILS MOMENT

SCAGLIONE JR.: "I'm going to stick with the theme of this game for this moment. As I mentioned, the one moment is with Brian Boyle and his son Declan. After the Devils won that game, the clock struck zero and the team gathered around Keith Kinkaid. Travis Zajac and Andy Greene went to center ice and hugged. They were the only remaining players on the roster who played with the Devils in the 2012 playoffs, so this was particularly special for those two. And from my perspective, I remember watching Travis and Andy come up as rookies in the 2006-07 season.

"That was the last season at the Meadowlands. So these were two players who came up as rookies and in their first couple of years in the league, as Andy Greene said to me, 'it wasn't a matter of making the playoffs those years. It was, we knew we were going to make the playoffs and we knew we were going to have home ice advantage. It was a matter of where we were going to be seeded when the season finished; first, second, third or fourth?'

"And then, for those two, they went from a perennial playoff team, Cup contender, to a team that got to the Stanley Cup Final, two wins away from winning the Stanley Cup and in some respects two goals away, if you just flip the results of Games 1 & 2, which they lost in overtime to Los Angeles. To then going through this playoff drought the next several years. And not just that. These two players had been through an ownership change from Jeff Vanderbeek to Josh Harris and David Blitzer. These two had been around since Lou Lamoriello. Lou drafted Zajac and Greene was signed as a college free agent. And God only knows how many coaches they had been through up until that point.

"They had been through almost everything at that point. And now that they were able to go back to the playoffs, where they were still used to being at the beginning of their careers, it was a special moment."

18 JIM SULLIVAN (ICE OFFICIAL)
THE MYSTERIOUS YELLOW SUNDAY INCIDENT (@BRENDAN
BYRNE ARENA)
MAY 8, 1988
NJD 3, BOS 1

BACKGROUND

If you grew up in Brooklyn, New York, during the middle of the 20th Century, or even the latter half of the century, there's a very good chance you were exposed to a variety of sports. And while Brooklyn has a very rich history of producing professional athletes, as well as writers and broadcasters, the borough has also produced quite a few league officials; across various sports, of course.

And one of the best to come from Brooklyn is a man by the name of Jim Sullivan.

Sullivan grew up playing roller hockey in the streets of Brooklyn, before eventually taking to the ice around the age of 17. And while he didn't make it to the NHL as a player, he DID make it to the NHL as an Off-Ice Official.

JIM SULLIVAN: "Well, I was involved in hockey all my life. I played and later on, I became a ref. I was the ultimate rink rat. I was in a rink seven days a week. When I got out of high school, I worked in a rink full-time, not that it was going to be a career, but I was a young kid. I didn't go to college, unfortunately. And hockey was always my favorite sport, even though I grew up in Brooklyn when no one played, or very few people played. Basketball was always the big sport in Brooklyn. I got involved with hockey, believe it or not, just by looking at maybe magazines and pictures and by listening to games on the radio and then when TV first came in.

"I have no idea why I liked it. No one in my family ever played. It's not like today, where my son plays, my grandsons play. A couple of my granddaughters even played, because they grew up with me with the hockey. And they grew up with the Islanders. But it was just something that I liked. I couldn't explain it. I started my own team on the block in Brooklyn. Then I went to the park and played. I didn't put ice skates on until I was 17. I used to play roller hockey everyday after school, until it got dark. And then, all day, Saturday and Sunday. But once I put on ice skates, that was it, no more roller hockey.

"I was a Rangers fan and then my favorite player, Ron Murphy, got traded to Chicago, so I became a Chicago fan, as kids will do. He wasn't a superstar. He was just an average player.

"Then, in the mid-1960s, one of my closest friends in the world, was a TV director and he was the Rangers practice goalie. They only had one goalie. So he would practice with the team maybe four or five days a week and he would be at the home games. So he said to me, 'the Rangers were looking for some new guys (to be Off-Ice Officials).' Some of the older guys were retiring and he said, 'I'll recommend you.'

"I said, 'I had just joined the NYPD and I was working around the clock. I had absolutely no seniority as far as switching tours. I had one small child and another one on the way. I wouldn't have had any use for the tickets. And I would have missed an awful lot of the games and I just couldn't commit.' So, when the Islanders came in, in 1972, this same guy was now directing and he asked if I was interested. By then I had enough seniority where I could switch my tours around and everything.

"My kids were a little bit bigger so they could use the tickets. And he said to me, 'they were having a meeting that night. So if I had waited another day to let him know I was interested, I might not have gotten picked.' So I went to the meeting and I knew most of the people. I knew to supervisor and one of the Rangers Off-Ice Officials, who was helping to get the crew started. He recommended me. So that's how I started with the NHL."

That's quite a journey for a humble man from Brooklyn, but it's one he enjoyed. And still does.

JIM SULLIVAN: "Usually, I was the assistant scorer, but I would also be the assistant statistician, which they don't have anymore. Back then, they had the books. Now, of course, they have computers. And occasionally I would be the assistant timekeeper and occasionally I would run the clock. For 12 years I was a spare. I did whatever was needed and then I became the official scorer. I was the official scorer for my last 32 years. I did other things, but I would say 95% of the time, or maybe even more, I was the official scorer. I probably scored a thousand games.

"Each team has its own crew (and I was primarily with the Islanders). But up until about maybe 10 to 15 years ago, they would use neutrals for the playoffs. So they would send you out of town and you never knew where you'd be going. I mean, they'd keep you fairly local, but it was a blast."

It was such a blast that Sullivan still keeps himself active in hockey by playing on a men's league team. And remember, he's currently doing this while also being in his late-80s! Sometimes, you just love something so much that you just have to keep going. And going.

MOST UNFORGETTABLE DEVILS GAME

Whenever you talk about craziness in sports, hockey isn't far from the conversation. From the Stanley Cup being left on the side of the road, to brawls that saw players fighting through the stands where the fans were sitting, hockey has seen it all.

And by the time the NHL was nearly 80-years-old, many thought they had indeed seen everything there was to see in Hockey. That is, until a Referee and a Head Coach had a spat that lead to legal action and necessitated a trio of replacement Ice-Officials to officiate a Stanley Cup playoff game. Oh, and for good measure, it was Mother's Day.

You might ask, "What game am I talking about?" The answer. I'm talking about the still mysterious "Yellow Sunday" incident, better known as the, "Have Another Donut" incident.

In the spring of 1988, the New Jersey Devils were on a Cinderella run, having qualified for the playoffs for the first time in team history. And after dispatching the Islanders and the Capitals, they were just four wins away from their first ever appearance in the Stanley Cup Final. However, one team stood in their way.

The Boston Bruins.

After splitting the first two games up in Boston, the series shifted to New Jersey, but the Devils' momentum did not. The Garden Staters lost Game 3 by the score of 6-1 and afterwards Head Coach Jim Schoenfeld got into an altercation with Referee Don Koharski.

While there is some dispute as to exactly what happened, this much is clear. Schoenfeld was chirping about the way Koharski and his crew had officiated Game 3. And Koharski, rather than walk away, chose to engage Schoenfeld, thus escalating the situation.

Now here's where the details get sketchy.

Depending on who you believe, Koharski either tripped or Schoenfeld pushed him down. And at some point, Schoenfeld yelled at Koharski, "You're crazy, you're crazy. You fat pig. Go have another doughnut."

Well, that whole incident, which should have been avoided, landed Schoenfeld a one-game suspension from the league. And his suspension meant that he would not be able to be behind the bench for Game 4. However, the Devils sought and received an injunction from a New Jersey Judge.

Are you with me so far? Good, because things are about to get crazy.

When the Ice-Officials found out that Schoenfeld was free to coach that night, they decided they would not officiate the game. Under normal circumstances, things might have been handled better. But this was the playoffs and, of course, League President, John Ziegler was nowhere to be found.

So what do you do? They couldn't cancel the game. But you need referees and linesmen to officiate a game, especially one as important as this.

Luckily, there happened to be a trio of Off-Ice Officials in the building and they were about to become the main characters in this circus.

Paul McInnis, Vince Godleski and Jim Sullivan were approached by the league's Director of Officiating, John McCauley, whose son Wes is currently a beloved NHL referee, about possibly going out on the ice as the replacement officials.

JIM SULLIVAN: "They kind of picked the three of us. I had worked a lot of games that year and one thing that they probably noticed was that all three of us were in pretty good shape. I was 51, Vinny was 51 and I think Paul was 52.

"So John said, 'would you guys want to do it?' I said, 'Well, would there be any repercussions?' And he said, 'there could be, but it's your call.' So we all looked at each other and said we'd do it. That was when they were still kicking it around, not ever thinking that it was going to happen.

"Really, up until the time we started to walk out onto the ice, I thought this thing was going to get worked out.

"They had put us in a basketball locker room for an hour; they didn't want us near the regular referees, for obvious reasons. It was like going into the electric chair. They got us some makeshift equipment. Then the Trainer came in with some Devils practice jerseys, which were black. But the Bruins wore black so we couldn't wear them.

"So we waited there and got dressed. And at that point, the game was already an hour past it's supposed start time. Then, John McCauley walked in and we started going over a little bit of a game plan. And then he said, 'okay boys, go get them.'

"I should mention, Vinny had his own equipment in his car, but Paul and I didn't have anything with us. They gave us some light shin guards left over from the morning skates, but we had nothing for our thighs or anything like that. And we also had to borrow skates. And let me tell you, you can't really skate in borrowed skates.

"So we got out there and I was feeling a bit nervous, especially skating around in somebody else's skates. Plus, they gave us these mustard yellow jerseys to wear, which is why it was called, 'Yellow Sunday.' And I was embarrassed because I had always been considered a good skater, but if you watched on television, it looked like I could hardly skate. That's the problem with using skates that aren't yours.

"We got out on the ice and the players were cheating on every face-off. But other than that, the game was moving along. I missed one call on an off-sides during the first period, but otherwise I felt like I was doing alright."

While Sullivan and company were doing their best to make the game run as normal as possible, there were still some dust ups. And some goals. The Devils came out of the gate quickly and netted a 2-0 lead as Dave Maley and Pat Verbeek scored 45 seconds apart midway through the first period.

JIM SULLIVAN: "Finally, after the first period, they managed to get us some referee jerseys. And then we just went back out there and continued to do what we needed to do. I remember though, there were a couple of fights. At the time I was 195 pounds, but you have to realize, these guys were half my age and were professional athletes. So the fights were a bit of a problem. And the whole thing was, Paul, Vinny and I didn't want to determine the outcome of the game.

"We didn't want the game to be won or lost on our mistake. Anyway, the Devils won 3-1 to tie the series and honestly, I don't think the outcome would have been any different had the regular referees been out there. Which is exactly how we wanted it to be."

Talk about a crazy game and crazy situation. Never before had something like this happened in the NHL and hopefully it never will again.

MOST UNFORGETTABLE DEVILS MOMENT

SULLIVAN: ""In the regular season, I'd probably worked 50-100 Devils games throughout my career. However, the (Stephane) Matteau game was, not only the best Devils game, but the best hockey game, I ever saw in my life -- in person. I remember I scored that game and the seats where we sat in The Garden were right under the Blue Seats, which at that time were pretty raunchy. And I remember the Devils pulled their goalie and the fans were so close to us. I remember this one woman going, 'THEY SCORED?!' (After Valeri Zelepukin tied it with 7.7 seconds to go).

"That game just had everything. And at the time, whoever won that series was going to play Vancouver. Now, just about everybody figured the Devils or the Rangers would beat Vancouver for sure, which they did, although it took seven games. So, that was not only a great hockey game, but it was a huge hockey game. I've seen probably 2,000-hockey games in-person between my time in the NHL and when I was a fan for a lot of years. And that was probably the best game I'd ever seen."

MESSAGES TO DEVILS FANS

LARRY BROOKS: "The Devils were always a much stronger organization than they're given credit for. Always. Always a more involved fan base than they're given credit for. I don't really have any connections there at this point. Everyone I knew who worked there is gone, I think. But it's an organization, a franchise with a great history. And I know how important it is to hockey fans in New Jersey. I just, I do, because I lived it for nine years and I'm sure that hasn't changed.

"So, Ray (Shero) will get them back and they'll be a vibrant franchise. It's always better for hockey when all three teams (Devils, Islanders and Rangers) are good. It's always better for hockey in New York when all three teams are good. When they get back there, they'll get back there. We did pretty well back in the Meadowlands, it was always a well run organization."

STEVE CANGIALOSI: "Here's what I would say. You are growing in numbers. For the longest time I think we struggled to define what the Devils fan is. Okay. Because I think, when the team was born, you are the New Jersey Devils, but you have to win over the state of New Jersey. You have to remember; there was a deep hockey history in the area before you ever were the new kid on the block. So from Day One of your existence, you had to live in the shadow of the team that played in the big city. Okay. But there has been a process, a process that's better than three decades old now and a process that's going to continue for a very long time.

"Where I think the sons and daughters of good hockey fans, regardless of what team they might've rooted for in the '80s and '90s, are now coming of age. Their sons and daughters will come of age with this team that already has a great history, but the history is going to be likely enriched all the more as we move on with a different level of talent and different players that come in. And I think the timeless message would probably be this, as we continue this process, your days as the redheaded stepchild are going to wither away. That's what I would say."

KEN DANEYKO: "Oh Gosh, well, probably first and foremost thank you for the support and without the fans we're nothing. That has always been my motto since I was 19 years old, coming into the league, till right now, as far as being in the organization, 35, 36 years later is and they are part of the team. They're the sixth; they call it the sixth man in Basketball. I don't know what they call it in Hockey, but they are so important and I love making believe they're part of our team. And the support personally for me, on and off the ice, over the years. I had such a great relationship and a lot of that with the fans and I've always believed it and said it because I was a blue collar guy who believed in doing whatever it took to help the team win.

"And then I was one of those guys who just, the work ethic and I think the state of Jersey is like that and the Devils fans could relate to that. And that's kind of how, I still don't know who gave me the name, Mr. Devil. I'm not sure who gave me that. I think it was the fans in general. And I was much appreciative. I thought it was kind of funny at first. I didn't know if it was going to stick or whatever, but I'm honored and grateful because the fans could relate to me and that's something that I'm always going to cherish till the day I die. Certainly the Devils and the fans have been my second family, maybe my first; probably my 1A. But, I can't thank them enough for what they've done for me, for my career. More importantly for the team and the franchise in general."

JOHN DELLAPINA: "I grew up in New York, so I'm a parochial New Yorker, but I also spent 25 years living in New Jersey and raised my kids there. New Jersey is a special place. And I think when you're a Devils fan; you need to take pride in the fact that they are New Jersey's professional sports team. The Nets have come and gone. The Football teams play there, but they don't have that state name on their helmets. They are and you should be proud of that. And it's easy for me to say, as a New Yorker, but it's not about how many the other guys won or did they get more coverage?

"It's about New Jersey is a really cool place to live and work and be. And that's where Bruce Springsteen is from. I mean that's where Frank Sinatra is from. And that's the Devils. You should be proud of it. And it's a legacy locally. You have to go back to the Islander dynasty to have anything like what the Devils did in the mid-90s to the mid-2000s. They were a quasi dynasty in the NHL."

ROLAND DRATCH: "Well, I would say this, if I never produced another game, I would want to thank every Devils fan, no matter how old they are, boys, girls, men, women, doesn't matter. Without their support our show wouldn't be what it is. I mean, going back to different things, I know there's always been an argument about Devils fan saying we don't have as many Devils fans as this team or that team. But I'll say this; they're as passionate as any group I've ever seen.

"When we created things like Matt and The Maven and Chico Eats and other things, they took it to another level. They ran with it. And their support is just amazing. So what I would say to them is that I'm sure, if it was 15 to 20 years from now, a telecast without fans is no telecast. And the reason why our telecast is so good is because of them. And the telecast 20 years from now will be great because of Devils fans."

MIKE "DOC" EMRICK: "I said this at a couple of fan club meetings, because the Devils Fan Club has been -- the first meeting I attended, Ed Nudge was the President and we met at the Holiday Inn at Totowa. And then at subsequent meetings, Trudy Stetter was this very loyal President for a number of years. And we had meetings at various places and they were always such a loyal group. And occasionally when the Devils were going so well, I would say, there are times when it's just good to forget the pursuit and be happy because the team would be in such a good state and all of us who are fans of a team can always be the carnivorous about wanting one more win or winning one more, having one more seven game winning streak.

"But I think, appreciating when things are good and saying this is just great right now, isn't it? And recognizing that sports are cyclical and that there are times in the history of every team, even the Montreal Canadiens and even the New York Yankees, when there are going to be down times. And so sports is a cycle and all of the agonizing and all of this sweat, which all of us fans of a sports team go through, won't force anything to happen any faster. So there are times that we have to, in the pursuit of happiness, just sit and be happy. And there are times when we are going through agonizing times that we just have to be patient. I guess that would be my message, but the overriding message of it all is, because of those meetings in Totowa and because of those meetings with

Trudy and her group in various other parts of New Jersey, just thanks for the loyalty to the team all of those years."

STAN FISCHLER: "I've always admired the Devils fans because of their loyalty and passion and the fact that through many, many tough years, and I'm talking about when they came into the league, '82-'83 no playoffs, '83-'84 no playoffs, '84-'85 no playoffs, '85-'86 no playoffs -- that's suffering. '86-'87 no playoffs. And remember, in '87-'88, Doug Carpenter was the coach and he had been the coach for a while and he failed to get them into the playoffs. And I remember a big game at Madison Square Garden in December, very, very big game. And Lou (Lamoriello) had moved in as G.M. And I said to myself, cause I had lunch with Lou about a month before and he asked me what I thought of the team and he asked me what I thought of the coach and I said, 'I reserve judgment for a month. I want to see what happens in a month.' When the month was up, they got killed by the Rangers at The Garden, something like 9-3. And that's how Carpenter got the hook after Christmas and Schoenfeld got the job.

"It was very, very exciting. But what was so pleasing is how the fans supported the team and how in the worst conditions, including the Blizzard Game, these people showed up. It was unbelievable. And of course the cherry on top of the cake was The Cup win. The Cup win epitomized everything about the fans because this was an underdog team going into The Final against Scotty Bowman's Red Wings and guys in Canada were predicting that it would be four straight for Detroit. One wise guy wrote that it would be three straight for Detroit and they'd forfeit the fourth game. So the team was steadfast. The fans are steadfast. And now you've got a team in a beautiful arena in Newark, which was another thing a lot of people thought would never happen. So the fans have been very, very special and never stopped supporting the team in the worst of times and finally got their reward. And they have one of the best Fan Clubs in Hockey. They've been around a long time, have their own newspaper and they go on trips. I remember being with them in Ottawa for that terrific series. We beat the Senators in seven. They're very good fans."

ANDREW GROSS: "What I found when I took the Devils beat and again I'd been with the Rangers essentially from 2003 to 2015, so I had been with that franchise for a long-time covering them and coming over to the Devils, what I was immediately struck by was just, it's certainly not as big a fan base as the Rangers fan base is, but if anything it is more vocal and it's more crazed and it's more, I don't want to say more loyal because that's not fair because Rangers fans are loyal, but I had more interactions I think in the year and seven-eighths or whatever it

142

was covering the Devils then I did in 12 years with the Rangers. And I met a lot of nice people on the Rangers beat, but it seemed instantaneous, like the whole Devils Nation suddenly knew that I was taking over for Tom Gulitti. And as a writer, I sort of enjoy being somewhat anonymous.

"I don't expect everyone to know who I am and it was really weird the first few games I'm covering at The Rock, to walk around and hear, 'Oh that's Andrew Gross, he's taking over for Tom Gulitti.' So I guess my message for the Devils fans is really just, never lose that. I mean they have a really special relationship with their team and it's a relationship I really enjoyed being a part of because it was, to me, it seemed much more, mom and pop-ish in a way. The fans really felt like these were almost their kids playing for them. Like you were going to see a peewee game. It was the same kind of passion for the players and I really, really enjoyed that. It was very much a family atmosphere around that team. I've found that really, really neat and I hope that never goes away."

LARRY HIRSCH: "New Jersey Devils hockey, was the first major league team to arrive in New Jersey. Now the misnomer is that New Jersey is part of the New York metropolitan area. This is what Mr. McMullen didn't like. New Jersey is a separate state, you pay a lot of money to go over the George Washington Bridge or the Holland Tunnel or the Lincoln Tunnel. When you go to New Jersey you're in a different state. So this team was its first Major League team, in a brand new building, the Brendan Byrne Arena, and the Meadowlands also, in that whole complex that was built over there and then eventually got the Giants over there. And then the Jets and the Racetrack, it was all big.

"And so this is the first Major League team in New Jersey. And it will always be the first Major League team. They are not the New York Devils. Not the New York Islander Devils. Not the Connecticut Devils. They're the New Jersey Devils and it's New Jersey's team. Even the Giants and Jets are not New Jersey's teams. They originated in New York. They moved over. They are, along with Rutgers and soccer teams and everything, a New Jersey franchise and this was the first one. And fans can't forget that. And also fans can't forget that when they won the Stanley Cup championship, beating the Detroit Red Wings in '94-'95 there was controversy, because McMullen was kind of going back and forth in negotiations with the New Jersey Sports and Exposition Authority for a new lease and whatever. And he threatened to move the team to Nashville.

"Eventually, Nashville got a franchise. But there was that, 'well, if I'm not gonna get it, I'm moving.' There was that threat and I'll never forget, I was in the Devils' dressing room after they won The Cup, The Cup is there and the Governor of New Jersey, she was outside the Devils' dressing room. I went up to her, I introduced myself. Here's what I did and I said, 'Madame Governor, the most important thing you can do for the state, one of them anyway, is you've got to keep this team here. You can't let this team go because you and the state of New Jersey will live with that stigma for the rest of your life. You may not be a sports fan or whatever,' and she goes, 'oh no, I love the Devils.' 'Okay, then don't let this team go because you'll never live it down.'

"I meant it and that's probably the biggest message I can give. No matter how they're doing, good, bad or indifferent. This is your team; this is your franchise and root with it. Cheer when the good times are going. Say next year is another year, that type of thing. Right now they're in a transitional period with probably one of the best General Managers in Ray Shero. This guy is going to rebuild this franchise. And why do I say that? Because he won a championship in Pittsburgh. You know how tough it is to win the Stanley Cup. I saw it with my team, the Tampa Bay Lightning, when they learned that lesson this year and got eliminated in the first round after winning the President's Trophy.

"So that's the thing, New Jersey, this is your team. Covet it, embrace it, support it and don't let it ever, ever, slip out of your sports mind. And they have, I mean, they've embraced it. That's the biggest message I can give, because all of us that started this franchise, sold seats and everything like that. We know it will succeed because hockey is a great game. And as Phil Esposito once said, 'once you go to your first game, we've got you.' So that's how you build this franchise. Everybody likes a winner, I understand that. Look when the Devils were rolling and winning Stanley Cups, oh my God. But when you fall in, it's really when you fall in the hole a little bit and you have some dry years that you really test it. But I always say, I always like to see the flowers blossom. I always like to see the young players come in from the draft and everything and see the rebuilding of a club that has to be done.

"Ray has a tough job because when the key came after (Lou) Lamoriello, the cupboards were pretty bare and he didn't have much to work with and he didn't have an economic position to do that. He had to start all over. And amazingly, after his first two years there, he made the playoffs last year (2017-18). Nobody expected them to make the playoffs. They didn't have a good year this year, because last year's team, I think, overachieved and did well, but the higher expectations, it didn't follow that. So that's what happened this year. Ray is smart and Ray will rebuild the Devils. And I predict, with Ray and whomever, they will one day do the same thing they did at the Meadowlands and that's raise the Stanley Cup. And New Jersey deserves it."

MATT LOUGHLIN: "You were part of something special. You're an organization that came from two cities actually, Kansas City and Denver, but found a home in New Jersey and became an elite, respected franchise led by Hall of Famers. And not just Hall of Famers, but All-Time Hall of Famers in Scott Stevens and Marty Brodeur. No knock at Scott Niedermeyer, but if he did just a little bit more sometimes he might be one of the All-Time greats. But there's no question Stevens and Marty take their place at the top of that Hall of Fame Mountain.

"So you are a part of something good and real in Jersey and it's our thing and the red and black and the Christmas tree colors are all part of that and will never go away. And you have every right to put your chest out and say, I am a Devils fan. That's it. I mean Lou (Lamoriello) put this team on the map. Lou made being a Devils fan important and satisfying and this ownership group now is going to continue that and there's going to be ups and downs. But the Number One thing is just this organization. This organization has some history that makes it very special. Three championships, five appearances, more good things on the way. And again, everyone from that first year fan to somebody more recent is a part of something special."

COREY MASISAK: "I believe that the Devils fan base is inarguably one of the most unique in the league. And I believe that for a number of reasons. They, because of the Rangers and the relationship that Devils fans have with Rangers fans and because of being New Jersey's professional sports team, being in a market where other media outlets sometimes forget about them. And also just having an incredible amount of success for a franchise that whenever it started out, I mean, the most famous thing that was associated with it was, the Wayne Gretzky thing.

"To go from that to being one of the most successful franchises in the sport. It's just, the whole experience of the New Jersey Devils has been a pretty unique one, I think, in the NHL's history. And, it's a different kind of fan base than I've seen maybe in Pittsburgh or Washington. But it's just been an incredibly passionate one and I don't think that's going to change. I mean the franchise came along and they had success and that sort of planted the roots of everybody's fandom in New Jersey. I think that, for generations to come, they're going to build off of that."

MIKE MORREALE: "My message is, the best is yet to come. The Devils drafted a two-way phenomenon and in Nico Hischier two years ago. He's going to be a top one center in this league for so many years. They got the Number One pick in the draft this year in Jack Hughes. This is an elite, elite skater and playmaker. I am so excited to see how the Devils work with Nico Hischier and Jack Hughes for so many years -- 15 to 20 years. Ray Shero has done this before. Defensively, they're strong. Ty Smith and other good young players are going to be with this organization for a very long time.

"And I think goaltender Mackenzie Blackwood looks like he's going to serve as a backup to Cory Schneider and Blackwood is a player that eventually will take over the Number One reigns. I think he really proved himself. While we've only qualified for the playoffs once in the past six years, I think there's a lot to look forward to because once the Devils do get their stride and everything starts to come together, I think this is a team that's perennially going to be a perennial Stanley Cup contender and not just the playoff contender."

DEB PLACEY: "I would say, the thing that struck me from the first time I went to the arena to cover a game and to broadcast a game, that I always come back to is I was struck by all the families in the stands. It's really a generational audience in that there were The Cup years, because the Devils were an expansion franchise they don't go back a 100 years. But when you go back to their first decade of winning under Lou Lamoriello and with Marty Brodeur, Scott Niedermeyer, Scott Stevens and Patrik Elias, who came for the second one, but that group, Bill Guerin, Claude Lemieux, the generation of Devil fans then had kids and they started to come to games.

"And I think they will take their kids to games. It's a real family atmosphere and I think that that's what carries the Devils into the next generation. I think that's what makes the Devils unique in the metropolitan area in that, because they were a relatively new franchise, it's really a family following, if that makes sense. And I see moms and girlfriends and daughters and a lot of girls at the games. And I see boyfriends and girlfriends and grandparents and fathers and sons and they seem to share Devil games as a family. And I think that's what the Devils fans seem to me to be."

GLENN "CHICO" RESCH: "I didn't just make lifelong fans, I made lifelong friends right from that first year who I still see and interact with today. And I think that was the beauty of playing then, because you had to go to your car and you had to walk through the stands and they were waiting and they were talking to you. There wasn't any separation. And we became friends. The Devils fans became friends of mine and I think that, for me, fans are fans, but if they also become the player's friends, it makes it even more special. And I think that's one of the real warm parts of what I got out of playing in New Jersey, mainly because we were both in the same boat.

"They were fans who didn't have much respect because they were cheering for a losing team and we were the team that lost a lot. So we were struggling for our respect and it was just a special bond for me with the early Devils fans. And it still is today when I do TV or radio. I just love getting to know something about the fans. Don't ask me why, but it's just fascinating. And I have found, if I let them talk and I asked them questions, it's just amazing the warm stories you get. So, for me, that would be the message, fans, you really matter. Fans can help get you through really tough moments because they stay loyal and fans can take teams to a higher level."

CHRIS RYAN: "I think regardless of the players wearing the uniform that they all respect and honor the tradition that this team has built. I mean, they came here; they were essentially built out of nothing when they arrived in New Jersey. They battled to just make the playoffs in the late-'80s and turned into a three-time Cup champion. And even though a lot of that history has changed and like you said, the people and players have changed. That tradition hasn't gotten. And I think the players, they say it a lot. They play for the logo on the chest and guys like Travis Zajac and Andy Greene, they go back to kind of that last generation and they're the last connections to it and they've never lost that message and they've kind of passed it on.

"I think that's what you see over the course of the franchise, no matter how many different owners, coaches, players, managers come in, that's kind of a lasting message and it carries on and I think that's on the players in the room to ultimately do that. You see these guys play with pride as lifelong Devils and they carry that through and a lot of young players in the room look up to them. And I think that's going to continue in terms of the tradition of the team and people always playing for the logo and understanding what kind of history the Devils have, even for a smaller team."

BRYCE SALVADOR: "Well I just want to thank the Devils fans for really supporting the players, like myself, during the time they've had here. And the seven years that I had with the Devils, just the support through the ups and the downs. It's remarkable when you have a fan base that is so passionate about their team and they come and support them. Even though they've won three Cups, not too many organizations can say that. And yet they're there all the time and through different turmoil, whatever it may be, whether it's moving to a new rink or changing of General Managers, coaches, in the playoffs, not in the playoffs. It's just;

they're always there. And the support is appreciated so much by all the players and the organization.

"It's a testament to them and how passionate they are about the Devils fan and about the Devils players themselves. It wasn't something that I was expecting when I got traded here. And even for players like myself who have transitioned and are still around the Devils in the communities and just how they continue to support the alumni is second to none. It's remarkable. It's what makes them such a special group of fans. I just want to say, don't lose that passion. Don't lose that fight because that's what makes them really special and unique."

LEO SCAGLIONE JR.: "Stay passionate. It's a very special fan base in the sense that you're cheering for a team, the only team in pro-sports that associates itself with New Jersey. So, if you're a Devils fan in New Jersey, in the Garden State, that's special. With the Giants or the Jets or the Red Bulls you're cheering for a team that has a home base in New Jersey, but they still associate themselves with New York. So it's stay passionate. You're also surrounded by too loud, crazy fan bases right to the north of you in New York and then south of you in Philadelphia.

"So you're right in the middle of these two. And then you have your own team, which has been the more successful team of any of the local teams for the past 20 years. You've been through a lot, you've seen a lot. Stay passionate, stay loud. I can remember games in the old arena, standing in the upper concourse and the building was rocking -- it was shaking. It was exciting. Being at Prudential Center and covering his team, when that building gets loud it's one of the loudest buildings in the NHL. So keep it going."

JIM SULLIVAN: "Hockey runs in cycles. You had your day in the sun. You won your Cups. You had a great team, you had a great goaltender and I think better days are ahead. Your best player was out for a lot of the season with an injury and now you have a good draft pick coming in. So I think better days are ahead. I'm a great believer in, if you're a fan of a team, you stick with the team. I'm probably still a Brooklyn Dodgers baseball fan. I believe in loyalty. No team stays on top forever anymore. So you stick with your team. Your loyalty. Your team. There are better days ahead but you take the good with the bad."

ACKNOWLEDGEMENTS

For those who think that writing a book is easy, it's not. And you need more than just yourself to finish such a project. Therefore, it's important to thank those who have helped you along the way. So, I would like to acknowledge the following people for their roles in this project.

Larry Brooks, Steve Cangialosi, Ken Daneyko, John Dellapina, Roland Dratch, Mike "Doc" Emrick, Stan Fischler, Andrew Gross, Larry Hirsch, Matt Loughlin, Corey Masisak, Mike Morreale, Deb Placey, Glenn "Chico" Resch, Chris Ryan, Bryce Salvador, Leo Scaglione Jr. and Jim Sullivan all took time out of their busy schedules to be interviewed for chapters in this book and told their stories with the same enthusiasm they share with the fans while doing their jobs.

Pete Albietz and Dan Schoenberg helped provide access to the subjects of this book.

My parents -- Mandi and Seth -- sister -- Tara -- grandparents -- Morton, Stanley, Yvonne and Zella -- uncles -- Andrew, Lenny, Scott and Glenn -- and aunts -- Yvonne, Anita and Brooke -- all of whom provided support throughout the book writing process.

My friends -- Samantha Bruno, Deanna Chillemi, Brittany Ciraolo, Taylor Chiaia, Lauren DeCordova, Jessica DiMari, Leanna Gryak, Stef Hicks, Maria Koutros, Christina Luddeni, Arianna Rappy, Michele Rosati, Amanda Sorrentino, Jessica Sorrentino, Brianna Torkel,

Victoria Wehr, Maggie Wince, Jared Bell, Trevor Blenman, Andrew Bodnar, Skylar Bonné, Walt Bonné, Danny Randell, Bobby Denver, Robert DeVita, Brandon Dittmar, Jared Fertig, Landon Goldfarb, Daniel Greene, Peter Koutros, Michael Manna, Matt Mattone, Logan Miller, Mike O'Brien, Dan O'Shea, Reid Packer, Chris Pellegrino, Max Rappy, Jason Russo, Aaron Shepard, Anthony Spadaro, William Storz and Joey Wilner -- all of whom provided assistance and support throughout the book process as well.

And to my fellow media members/colleagues/etc. who have helped to guide and influence my career -- Kenny Albert, Jeff Beukeboom, Martin Biron, Josh Bogorad, Amanda Borges, Ryan Braithwaite, Brendan Burke, Matt Calamia, Rick Carpiniello, Scott Charles, Ryan Chiu, Hayley Cohen, Russ Cohen, Charlie Cucchiara, Jack Curry, John Davidson, Jeff Day, Bob de Poto, Rachel Schwartz Dixon, Ron Duguay, Chris Ebert, Katie Epifane McCarthy, Annie Fariello, John Fayolle, Jeff Filippi, Matt Fineman, Jim Fox, Jim Gallagher, John Giannone, Rod Gilbert, Butch Goring, Adam Graves, Shannon Hogan, Nick Holmer, Eric Hornick, Kelly Keogh, Rachel Krawsek, Allan Kreda, Don La Greca, Jon Lane, Paul Lauten, Jon Ledecky, Dave Maloney, Joel Mandelbaum, Dan Marrazza, Jim Matheson, Matt McConnell, Patrick McCormack, Kevin Meininger, Bob Melnick, Sal Messina, Joe Micheletti, Emma Miller, Bobby Mills, Lucky Ngamwajasat, Ryan Nissan, Michael Obernauer, Arda Ocal, Pat O'Keefe, Glenn Petraitis, Brad Polk, Michael Rappaport, Mike Richter, John Rosasco, Howie Rose, Dan Rosen, Sam Rosen, Mark Rosenman, Larry Roth, Samuel Sandler, Sarah Servetnick, Ashley Scharge, Arthur Staple, Derek Stepan, Colin Stephenson, Robert Taub, Al Trautwig, Leslie Treff, Steve Valiquette, Colleen Wagoner, Mollie Walker, Ryan Watson, Craig Wolff, Cory Wright, Steve Zipay and Alyse Zwick.

SOURCES

(n.d.). 1982-83 New Jersey Devils Roster and Statistics. Retrieved from
https://www.hockey-reference.com/teams/NJD/1983.html

(n.d.). 1985-86 New Jersey Devils Roster and Statistics. Retrieved from
https://www.hockey-reference.com/teams/NJD/1986.html

(n.d.). 1987-88 New Jersey Devils Schedule and Results. Retrieved from
https://www.hockey-reference.com/teams/NJD/1988_games.html

(n.d.). 1987-88 NHL Summary. Retrieved from https://www.hockey-
reference.com/leagues/NHL_1988.html

(n.d.). 1993-94 New Jersey Devils Roster and Statistics. Retrieved from
https://www.hockey-reference.com/teams/NJD/1994.html

(n.d.). 1994-95 New Jersey Devils Roster and Statistics. Retrieved from
https://www.hockey-reference.com/teams/NJD/1995.html

(n.d.). 1995-96 New Jersey Devils Roster and Statistics. Retrieved from
https://www.hockey-reference.com/teams/NJD/1996.html

(n.d.). 2011-12 New Jersey Devils Roster and Statistics. Retrieved from
https://www.hockey-reference.com/teams/NJD/2012.html

(n.d.). 2011-12 New Jersey Devils Schedule and Results. Retrieved from
https://www.hockey-reference.com/teams/NJD/2012_games.html

(n.d.). 2011-12 NHL Summary. Retrieved from https://www.hockey-
reference.com/leagues/NHL_2012.html

(n.d.). 2017-18 New Jersey Devils Roster and Statistics. Retrieved from
https://www.hockey-reference.com/teams/NJD/2018.html

(n.d.). Boston Bruins at New Jersey Devils Box Score - May 8, 1988. Retrieved from https://www.hockey-reference.com/boxscores/198805080NJD.html

(n.d.). Buffalo Sabres at New Jersey Devils Box Score - April 29, 1994. Retrieved from https://www.hockey-reference.com/boxscores/199404290NJD.html

(n.d.). Chicago Blackhawks at New Jersey Devils Box Score - March 17, 2009. Retrieved from https://www.hockey-reference.com/boxscores/200903170NJD.html

Cyrgalis, B. (2018, June 1). The Post's Larry Brooks voted into Hockey Hall of Fame. Retrieved from https://nypost.com/2018/06/01/the-posts-larry-brooks-voted-into-hockey-hall-of-fame/

(n.d.). Detroit Red Wings at New Jersey Devils Box Score - June 24, 1995. Retrieved from https://www.hockey-reference.com/boxscores/199506240NJD.html

Harrington, M. (2019, April 26). 25 years later, Dominik Hasek and Dave Hannan still marvel at Sabres' 4-OT win over Devils. Retrieved from https://buffalonews.com/2019/04/26/buffalo-sabres-dominik-hasek-nhl-new-jersey-devils-dave-hannan-martin-brodeur/

Morganti, A. (2018, September 3). DEVILS WIN AFTER OFFICIALS WALK OUT. Retrieved from https://www.chicagotribune.com/news/ct-xpm-1988-05-09-8803150685-story.html

(n.d.). New Jersey Devils at Buffalo Sabres Box Score - April 27, 1994. Retrieved from https://www.hockey-reference.com/boxscores/199404270BUF.html

(n.d.). New Jersey Devils at Chicago Blackhawks Box Score - April 3, 1988. Retrieved from https://www.hockey-reference.com/boxscores/198804030CHI.html

(n.d.). New Jersey Devils at Florida Panthers Box Score - April 26, 2012. Retrieved from https://www.hockey-reference.com/boxscores/201204260FLA.html

(n.d.). New Jersey Devils at New York Rangers Box Score - March 19, 2012. Retrieved from https://www.hockey-reference.com/boxscores/201203190NYR.html

(n.d.). New York Rangers at New Jersey Devils Box Score - April 3, 2018. Retrieved from https://www.hockey-reference.com/boxscores/201804030NJD.html

(n.d.). New York Rangers at New Jersey Devils Box Score - May 25, 2012. Retrieved from https://www.hockey-reference.com/boxscores/201205250NJD.html

(n.d.). New York Rangers at New Jersey Devils Box Score - November 2, 1985. Retrieved from https://www.hockey-reference.com/boxscores/198511020NJD.html

(n.d.). New York Rangers at New Jersey Devils Box Score - October 8, 1982. Retrieved from https://www.hockey-reference.com/boxscores/198210080NJD.html

(n.d.). Philadelphia Flyers at New Jersey Devils Box Score - November 11, 1995. Retrieved from https://www.hockey-reference.com/boxscores/199511110NJD.html

Stein, A. (2018, October 1). Hall Nets Overtime Winner In Switzerland. Retrieved from https://www.nhl.com/devils/news/hall-nets-overtime-winner-in-switzerland/c-300546080

(n.d.). Toronto Maple Leafs at New Jersey Devils Box Score - April 5, 2018. Retrieved from https://www.hockey-reference.com/boxscores/201804050NJD.html

***NOTE: All interviews were conducted either in-person or over the phone in order to obtain the necessary quotes and information.

ABOUT THE AUTHOR

Matthew Blittner, born and raised in Brooklyn, New York, has been covering the New Jersey Devils, New York Rangers and New York Islanders for multiple publications since the beginning of the 2016-17 NHL season. Along the way, he has covered each of the teams' respective playoff runs over the past three seasons.

Among the publications Matthew Blittner has written for are: MSGNetworks.com, The Fischler Report, The Hockey News Magazine and NY Sports Day.

In addition to his responsibilities covering the NY/NJ hockey scene, Matthew obtained his Master's Degree in Sports Management from CUNY Brooklyn College in February of 2017 -- graduating with Summa Cum Laude honors.

Matthew's latest book, Unforgettable Devils, details the most significant games and moments in the careers of the broadcasters and writers who have covered the team for generations.
Visit his Facebook page at
https://www.facebook.com/UNFORGETTABLEDEVILS/ or on Twitter @MatthewBlittner.

Made in the USA
Middletown, DE
19 September 2019